SPIRITUAL BATTLE RATTLE: GOD'S ARMOR
MILITARY VETERANS' REVIEW OF EPHESIANS 6:10-18

Edward L. Linebaugh, U.S. Army Retired

Publisher/General Editor/Contributing Author

Stay Spiritually Strong!

eel

Cover Design by Michael Advertising Group, Huntsville, AL

Front Cover Photo: Staff Sergeant Albert Flores, U.S. Army
Used by permission.

InLine Publishers, LLC
("InLine With God's Word")
P.O. Box 12793
Huntsville, AL 35815

TABLE OF CONTENTS

DEDICATION

FORWARD

PROLOGUE

CHAPTER ONE   GOD'S ARMY STRONG!

CHAPTER TWO   ARMOR-UP

CHAPTER THREE   MILITARY INTELLIGENCE

CHAPTER FOUR   WEB GEAR

CHAPTER FIVE   BOOTS ON THE GROUND

CHAPTER SIX   MISSILE DEFENSE

CHAPTER SEVEN   BONE DOME

CHAPTER EIGHT   WEAPON TRAINING

CHAPTER NINE   SECURE NETWORK

CHAPTER TEN   GUARD DUTY

EPILOGUE   SPIRITUALLY WOUNDED WARRIORS

ENDNOTES   WORKS CITED

APPENDIX A   MILITARY JARGON/ABBREVIATIONS

APPENDIX B   BIBLE VERSIONS/ABBREVIATIONS

DEDICATION

To our Supreme Commander-in-Chief, Almighty God
and to our Lord and Savior, Jesus Christ
through His Holy Spirit.
All glory and praise forever and ever.

This book is also dedicated to the following military ministries:

American Military Evangelizing Nations (Manchester, CT)
Military OutReach & Encouragement (Huntsville, AL)
Military Outreach Program (Denver, CO)

for their support and care of our

Soldiers, Sailors, Airmen, Marines, Coast Guardsmen, and Guardians,
as well as their families stationed or deployed throughout the world.

FORWARD

The Christian life is undoubtedly the absolute best existence one can choose to live. It is the "abundant life" (John 10:10) and, in fact, the only life which leads to everlasting life (Romans 6:20-22). That said, the Christian life is not always easy; it is in many ways challenging, even demanding. Jesus said there must be cross-bearing by those who would be His faithful disciples (Luke 9:23). Thus, Christians will face challenges and pitfalls along the way. Consequently, there will be various trials to face, and one's faith will be sorely tested (James 1:2-4). Personal and physical suffering, even persecution, is bound to come (Romans 5:3-5; 2 Timothy 3:12).

While every Christian will face these difficulties, challenges, and persecutions, those serving in the armed forces face distinctive challenges. Brothers and sisters wearing the uniform will deal with many circumstances and situations not faced by their civilian brethren. Military service places expectations and demands on its members, which require rigorous training; long, difficult duty days (often including weekends and holidays); extended periods of separation from family and friends; deployments to desolate, remote duty locations, and often in dangerous, hostile, life-threatening combat conditions.

Duty requirements make it challenging to find time for personal Bible study, prayer, and meditation, let alone affording time and opportunity to attend worship services and enjoy the fellowship of like-minded people. Peer pressure to be "one of the guys or gals" can be a strong temptation to fall into sinful practices. Constant exposure to vulgar language, cursing, worldly attitudes, bad behavior, and so on can wear down one's resistance to such things. Facing constant danger, violence, and other realities of hostilities and war can harden a person mentally and spiritually. I can empathize and know these things are spot-on as I write from a firsthand perspective. I also wore the soldier's uniform for nearly thirty years, and as one who continues to this day ministering to Christians in the military. Therefore, I know and understand the pressures, difficulties, and unique challenges and temptations Christians face in the military. In this regard, the editor of this book, Ed Linebaugh, has performed an excellent service for Christian men and women (and their families) serving in the military.

This book's theme, "Spiritual Battle Rattle: God's Armor" from Ephesians 6:10-18, is one of preparation, readiness, and diligence. It is a call to arms for faithful service in God's spiritual army. Paul's inspired writing regarding God's whole armor is the perfect text for challenging military members to train, prepare, endure, and don His "battle rattle" vital for this spiritual warfare. We all play a role. Ed assembled a SEAL

(spiritual education and leadership) Team of writers—a spiritual battle buddies group. These are men who are not only faithful Christians but men who themselves have "been there and done that." They have all worn the uniform: Army, Navy, Marines, and Air Force are all represented among these men. They, too, have experienced military life's hardships and demands, some even the horrors of combat. So, as you read each of these chapters, know that you are reading words written from a personal, "been there, done" that perspective." None of them are perfect warriors who got it all right. But you, the reader, can be assured of their genuineness and the truth of their message. Each brother deals with an element of Paul's text in Ephesians chapter six, giving it a detailed exposition. Then, often using their own military experiences, life application is clear and easily understood. I especially appreciate the effective use of military jargon and scenarios in making these points clear and understandable, especially to a military audience.

While Christians serving in the military face unique challenges and adversities, living a godly life can—and must—be achieved! Whether you are stationed aboard a ship at sea (on float), on an FOB in Afghanistan, an airbase in the CONUS, work behind a desk in the Pentagon, or work in a unit orderly room or motor pool, you can proudly serve in uniform and be a faithful Christian. But it will take courage, it will take discipline, it will take commitment, it will take deep

faith, and it will take resources. And so, I commend this volume—*Spiritual Battle Rattle: God's Armor*—as a helpful resource in your MOLLE or FILBE backpack system during tactical operations or your kit bag, backpack, or sea bag. If you read and apply its intended message to your personal and military life, I am confident that you will be both enlightened and encouraged as you "soldier-on" in service to your country and, more importantly, in serving our great Commander-in-Chief on high.

John Phillis

U.S. Army, Retired

Program Coordinator, Military Outreach

Albuquerque, New Mexico

Email: jphillis@comcast.net

PROLOGUE

"Finally, be strong in the Lord and in the strength of His might. Put on the full armor of God, so that you will be able to stand firm against the schemes of the devil." (Ephesians 6:10-11)

I have sought to author a book for eons that would appeal to the hearts and souls of Christian men and women serving in our U.S Armed Forces. While teaching college in 2007 (the same year our CINC ordered a surge of U.S. troops to Iraq), I started putting pen to paper and paused. I got as far as penning the outline, introduction, first (now chapter three) and last chapter before putting it all on the back burner due to other ministry commitments, time constraints, etc., and never got around to completing my quest. When I retired the second time in late 2018, I recruited a team of excellent brothers in Christ who have honorably served our country in uniform. Several were company and field grade officers, including a West Point graduate, while many were lower enlisted; several were, and are, senior noncommissioned officers (NCOs) or chief petty officer (CPO); all have worn or are wearing boots like yours (their ranks are purposely not used). Several of these men are now gospel preachers, one is a retired university professor; all are respected leaders in their congregations, all are

faithful servants, all have been tested and tried in spiritual combat, and all are heroes of the faith in God's Army. I am very blessed to have known most of them for several years, and two of them, John Phillis and Darren Crowden, since the Cold War days while stationed together in Europe. I cannot thank these men enough for sharing their collective experiences and insights into God's Word for their assigned chapter. I am indebted to each of you! *Shalom.*

Today's warfighter, whether serving inside or outside the "wire" (e.g., secure versus unsecured area) or deployed at sea, needs assurance that he or she is not alone on the battlefield and has the proper resources or equipment to sustain them for the fight. Just as a soldier or Marine's "battle buddy" or cohort responsible for watching each other's "back" or welfare, every Christian soldier needs a spiritual battle buddy to help protect them while engaging their Spiritual Enemy, the Devil. Moreover, Christians need to don or apply *every* piece—not half or three-quarters—of the battle gear from God's armory to sustain them for the good fight (2 Timothy 4:7).

Try to imagine any warfighter in Iraq, Afghanistan, or other future combat zones (i.e., Eastern Europe, Pacific Rim or other flashpoints) who says, "I don't need all this stuff, it's a hassle, it's not worth

carrying!" Crazy? Insane? Of course not! Hey, I want all the protection I can get from the bad dudes, don't you? Fellow troops, we are in a *spiritual* life and death conflict! Our eternal destinies and those of our beloved friends and family members are at stake! Our choice is *heaven* or *hell* with no other alternative. God calls us to faithfully engage our enemy in battle as full-time Active Duty soldiers of the Cross.

A "battle rattle" was first used during the American Civil War; it was …

> A device with a handle and a box which when spun would make a noise that could be heard above the sounds of battle. Used during the Civil War to inform sailors to board the opposing ship or all hands on deck to fight depending on the captain's orders. [It was] Also used in conjunction with a gong as another signal. [It was] clearly a sound that could be heard over the sound of battle. Device is on display in the Civil War Navy Museum, Columbus, GA. [1]

In more recent U.S. combat operations, "battle rattle" denotes military gear worn in combat. "Full battle rattle is close to 50 pounds worth of gear, including a flak vest, Kevlar helmet, gas mask, ammunition, weapons, and other basic military equipment … Wearing the battle rattle has saved lives in both Iraq and Afghanistan." [2] And so, the idea for the title of this book.

Whether you are a Soldier, Sailor, Airman, Marine, Coastguardsman, or Guardian (e.g., new Space Force member) serving on active duty, the Reserves, or in the Army, Air, or Space National Guard, you are a vital component of God's Army Strong! Every child of God is essential in His spiritual Army, whether serving in the U.S. military or not. We implore you to enlist and remain on spiritual active duty or deployment until our "Command-in-Chief" (Jesus Christ) makes His triumphant return (1 Thessalonians 4:16) or die while engaging the enemy (Revelation 14:13). There is no ETS or EAOS discharge or separation in God's Army (unless we choose to go AWOL—Absent Without the Lord), neither is there spiritual retirement in this life! There are also no reserve or guard units (once known as "weekend warriors") in Jehovah's Spiritual Forces awaiting activation. God's Army must be fit-to-fight to deploy when and wherever He orders, whether to work, school, or to an APO, DPO, or FPO address, meaning duty station overseas (or on the seas). Just as U.S. forces are ready to "fight tonight," [3] so God's Armed Forces must always be combat-ready.

Like our American military forces, every soldier of the cross must continuously train and fight to win over Satan and his evil forces. "A new book of advice for Afghanistan operations says soldiers should get plenty of battle-focused training to prepare them for the terrain …

Don't stop training just because you're in a fight. Incorporating training into the battle rhythm provides a forum to implement changes and gives teams and squads a chance to mentally reset." [4]

Invariably warfighters will suffer wounds on the battlefield (e.g., "wounded warriors"). Some sustain relatively minor injuries, while others suffer far more extensive physical trauma. Many combat-hardened soldiers and veterans suffer from combat-related trauma, affecting their hearts, minds, and souls. Post-traumatic stress disorder (PTSD) can also affect one's career, family, health, and so on unless promptly recognized and treated. Being wounded in spiritual combat can produce a unique kind of PTSD: Permanent or Temporary Setbacks or Defeats. If unrecognized or untreated, God's warfighter will succumb to the enemy's special weapons and tactics (SWAT) as described in the Bible. These spiritually wounded soldiers can, in turn, negatively influence their families, friends, and even churches.

It is our prayer that you will compare everything in this imperfect book with *the* Perfect Book—God's infallible word of truth, which will judge each person on the Last Day (John 12:48; Acts 17:11). May He richly bless your life and spiritual journey into eternity. *Hooah* (Army), *Oorah* (Marines), *Hooyah* (*Navy*), *Hoorah* (*Air Force*), and *Amen* (God's Army). Are you ready for Spiritual Battle? God's Army Strong! To Him be glory forever and ever! Let us hear from you!

Your fellow warfighter,

Ed Linebaugh
U.S. Army, Retired
Director, Military OutReach and Encouragement
Huntsville, Alabama
Email: more@minister.com

CHAPTER ONE

GOD'S ARMY STRONG!

"Finally, be strong in the Lord and in the strength of His might."
(Ephesians 6:10; All Scriptures hereafter are as noted.)

Before the "draft" officially ended on July 1, 1973, for the U.S. military and the start of an all-volunteer force, draftees, or conscripts—if qualified mentally and physically—were bound by law to serve in uniform whether they wanted to or not. Many fled to Canada or other countries as draft-dodgers, while others refused conscription and faced the penalty: serve your country or go to jail—many grudgingly raised their right hands and took the Oath. Nowadays, when a young man or woman desires to serve their country, they are not obligated as during the draft; instead, they make a conscious choice in swearing that sacred Oath of Enlistment or Commission (for officers). Thus, all enlisted personnel incur an eight-year military service obligation (MSO), a combination of active duty and inactive service, subject to recall during that time.

God's kingdom—the church—has a spiritual army composed of an all-volunteer force. Soldiers in His armed forces are neither drafted nor

conscripted against their will. When one chooses to obey the gospel of Jesus Christ and is baptized or immersed for the remission/forgiveness of their sins (Acts 2:37-41), God adds or assigns this saved soul to His church (Acts 2:47) and thus His "salvation army." Following the prophet Isaiah's heavenly vision, "I heard the voice of the Lord saying, 'Whom shall I send, and who will go for us? Then I said, 'Here I am! Send me'" (Isaiah 6:8, ESV). God was, and still is, looking for *volunteers*! When I picture this encounter between the Divine and mortal man, I see an excited individual ready to join God's Army Strong by raising his right hand and taking the spiritual Oath of Enlistment! There were no time limits or duration in Isaiah's enlistment contract—he was in it to win it—for life! How about you? Are you a spiritual patriot? Are you ready to "Be All You Can Be" (one of the Army's past recruiting slogans and one of my favorites) and experience the ultimate adventure and blessing this side of eternity?

Before we review our spiritual "battle rattle" or the "armor of God," let us first observe what the apostle Paul said before revealing the enemy before us and God's battle plan: "Finally, be strong in the Lord and in the strength of His might" (Ephesians 6:10). Why should we be *strong*—God's Army Strong? Just ask any Soldier (or Marine)! You cannot sit behind a desk or computer all day without getting stiff joints and a sore back (like some of us old grunts). A warfighter needs

2

regular physical training or conditioning to stay in shape: "More PT, Drill Sergeant, more P.T.!" If today's warriors do not maintain a daily exercise regimen, those hard-earned muscles from boot camp, basic combat training, or unit physical fitness begin to fade or waste away. In that case, they atrophy and become useless when trying to escape and evade enemy fire or capture.

Just as physical and mental stamina is crucial to battlefield survival, soldiers of Christ must remain strong *spiritually*. Being out of shape spiritually will cause a Christian warfighter to become a casualty of war (more about this in the Epilogue, "Spiritually Wounded Warriors"). Remaining God's Army Strong means being spiritually fit-to-fight and survive in any spiritual battlespace, whether OCONUS at base camps, night patrols in Afghanistan, in garrison in Germany, or the Republic of Korea (e.g., South Korea), on sea duty, or stateside/shore duty (CONUS or OCONUS). Our spiritual combat zone begins in our *hearts* and *minds* which, in turn, affect our daily lives; it will also impact our homes and family relationships, at school, and even in the church (the devil would have us believe otherwise).

Our strength or power is not intrinsic or from ourselves—it is totally from God Himself (remember, He is omniscient or all-powerful compared to weak, sinful human beings like ourselves). In the original Greek language, the word *strong* comes from "*dunamis*," [1] from which

our English word *dynamite* originates. If you have witnessed the destructive power of military-grade explosives hurling from a naval bombardment, or have experienced firsthand the brunt of an IED in Afghanistan or Iraq, then perhaps you will somewhat appreciate the analogy. The unleashing of the world's first and only detonation of a nuclear weapon that ended WWII in Japan was both staggering and horrendous in scope. (I visited Ground Zero at Hiroshima, Japan, in 2019, which was a very moving emotional experience.)

God's power—His *dynamic* force—is far above and beyond any human capability—His capacity is beyond superhuman (sorry Hollywood, there is no real Superman or Superwoman, nor any Superheroes. It's just you and me – mere mortals). A look at the creation account in Genesis chapter one reveals just how powerful God is: He spoke, and BAM! Everything came into existence according to His divine specifications or blueprint. Something from absolutely nothing! That, my friend, is God-power! But wait—there is something far more incredible!

Earlier in the letter to the church at Ephesus (in modern-day Turkey), Paul prays that his readers (you and I) "will understand the incredible greatness of God's power for us who believe him. This power is the same mighty muscle that raised Christ from the dead and seated him in the place of honor at God's right hand in the heavenly

realms" (1:19-20, NLT). When was the last time you fashioned something out of complete nothingness by mere mortal words? When did you ever bring a dead loved one back to life—by speaking three words or fewer (cf. Jesus raising Lazarus from the tomb: "Lazarus, come out!")? Me neither, nor will I try such an impossible feat because it would be useless.

Speaking of a power center, Redstone Arsenal in Huntsville, Alabama, was, until 2011, home to the U.S. Army's Explosive Ordnance Disposal School that produced various armaments since World War Two. It is now the main headquarters for many military and federal agencies: Army Materiel Command, Army Contracting Command, Army Security Assistance Command, Missile Defense Agency, National Aeronautics and Space Administration's Marshall Space Flight Center, and Federal Bureau of Investigation, and the Bureau of Alcohol, Tobacco, and Firearms (ATF). The National Center for Explosives Training and Research "investigates non-terrorism-related criminal acts involving explosives, bombings, and explosives threats." [2] Although they strive to limit the thunderous noise, it is commonplace to hear explosions day and night for miles away.

Just as being physically and mentally strong or healthy is not an option for today's military warriors, soldiers of Christ are to "be strong

in the Lord and His mighty power." The original language means to "receive or increase strength" and is an imperative – that is, a *command*, not an option. It is not a one-time action or activity in basic training or boot camp, nor is it P.T. twice a week in front of the barracks or on the parade field at o-dark hundred. Instead, it is in the *present* tense, meaning "occurring in actual time."

If I am weak spiritually, where do I appropriate this strength or power? Being God's Army Strong means being "in the Lord" (verse 10)—the only location where one can acquire spiritual *dynamite* or *explosive power* from God. How then does a person gain access "in the Lord"? It is through *immersion* or *baptism* into Christ: "For all of you who were baptized *into* Christ have clothed yourselves with [i.e., put on] Christ" (Galatians 3:27; Romans 6:23; emphasis added, *el*). Since Jesus Christ is Lord—meaning "despot or Master" (Acts 2:36; Romans 13:44), "clothe yourselves with Christ" is the same as "put on the Lord" in baptism. Thus being "in Christ" is equivalent to being "in the Lord." Being "in Christ" provides access to the spiritual benefits that Paul describes in the first chapter of Ephesians: (1) *adoption into God's family* [the church]; (2) *the gift of grace* [which he further describes in chapter two]; (3) *redemption* through the blood of Christ [as payment to forgive or pardon our sins]. Of paramount importance and eternal

6

value is the *spiritual battle rattle* or spiritual combat gear afforded to those baptized or immersed into Christ.

We can do the seemingly impossible with God's strength and power (Philippians 4:13). King David, himself a soldier and military commander, confidently said: "For by you I can run against a troop and by my God I can leap a wall" (Psalm 18:29). When we choose to place ourselves under the authority and control of another (hence, the meaning of "rank"), and in this case, God, we are assured ultimate victory – not just the overall war, but the individual daily skirmishes and battles. But preparation is *key*. As we train and arm ourselves from the divine armory, let us remember, "He trains my hands for battle, so that my arms can bend a bow of bronze. You have also given me the shield of Your salvation, and Your right hand upholds me; and Your gentleness makes me great. You enlarge my steps under me, and my feet have not slipped" (Psalm 18:34-36).

The expression "May the force be with you," made famous by the movie series *Star* Wars, is nothing compared to the spiritual strength available to God's soldier: "in the *force* [strength] of His *ability* [might]" (6:10). Hopefully, you can now better appreciate God's incredible power available to you in preparing for the inevitable spiritual battles we all face daily. Soldier on! ~ *EL*

SPIRITUAL
BATTLE BATTLE

How many of us, while growing up, have sung the song, "I'm in the Lord's Army"?

I may never march in the infantry,

Ride in the cavalry,

Shoot the artillery.

I may never fly o'er the enemy,

But I'm in the Lord's Army,

Yes, Sir!

This is an excellent song that contains many truths and recognizes that we are part of a great spiritual army, the most significant force in the universe—God's Army Strong!

Armies have existed almost from the beginning of time. People have striven to conquer other peoples and trained groups of soldiers to accomplish the same; conversely, other men have prepared to defend their homes and cities from defeat and destruction. Some people hate war and consider themselves pacifists. History demonstrates that countries with a well-trained military force have a much better chance of protecting their homelands and preserving peace.

SPIRITUAL

BATTLE

BATTLE

We see people who proclaim Christianity but do not understand (or appreciate and value) that we are a *family* who believes in one Lord, one faith, and one baptism (cf. Ephesians 4:5-6). God's family, the church, looks after one another, showing compassion, kindness, forgiveness, and love. However, we are more than a family—we are an Army of the Lord! Military ground forces begin with an individual, then serve in a squad, platoon, company, battalion, regiment, brigade, division, and a corps, "the largest tactical unit in the U.S. Army ... responsible for translating strategic objectives into tactical orders." [3] Similarly, in God's Army, His soldiers (Christians) serve as individuals, small groups, congregations large and small, and believers worldwide: a *brotherhood*.

While serving in the Air Force, I worked at the now-defunct George Air Force Base in California as an auto-pilot system technician; I also belonged to a squadron comprised of various repair groups and simultaneously a member of the Tactical Air Command. There were other commands such as the Strategic Air Command and Military Airlift Command. I say this to point out how important we are, individually, to the entire military command structure. Just as all military members play an essential role in our nation's collective defense, individual Christians are an indispensable part of serving in God's armed forces.

SPIRITUAL

BATTLE   BATTLE

We need to understand how important God felt that His people defend their homes and lands in Old Testament times. Through Moses, God told His people to be brave and courageous, that He would pave the way for them to defeat the enemy; however, they still had to go out and fight (Deuteronomy 31:6-7, 23). Moses led the Israelites in conquering the surrounding nations that were to the south and east of Canaan. In Numbers chapter 21, we read in the first few verses that the Canaanite King Arad had captured some Israelites. Israel made a vow to God that if He delivered them into their hand, the Israelites would destroy them, which is what they did. In verse 22 of that chapter, Israel sends messengers asking permission to go through their land. They would respect the Ammorite's sovereignty and go on to the king's highway, but Sihon, the king of Ammon, raised an army to fight Israel but was destroyed and lost cities to them. Later in the chapter, they faced Og, who was king of Bashan, who led his Army against Israel at Edrie (verse 33). Og, his sons, and his Army were all defeated, and their land given to Israel.

In Genesis 14:12, Abram (before God changed his name to Abraham) raised an army to rescue his nephew, Lot, who was taken captive. He found them and led an attack on their military at night by dividing his men into smaller groups and attacking and routing them when they did not expect any attack. In the book of Judges, we read

of many men and women who God called to lead their people to attack and overcome a foreign invader. We also find people like Gideon, Jephthah, and Deborah, who led Israel's armies against foreign aggressors. Moreover, we read of King David's innumerable victories. Second Samuel chapter eight details David's exploits over the Philistines, Moabites, Arameans, Syrians, and Edomites. In the previous chapter, we find where David settled into his palace and where the Lord gave him rest from all surrounding him. It is interesting (and sad) to read the final military conflicts that David faced were from his son, Absalom, and a man named Sheba, who led a revolt in 2 Samuel 20. This overall peace lasted for King David's later reign and his son, King Solomon's reign.

When God's people turned away from Him, He let other nations arise, challenge, and eventually overthrow and destroy them. For instance, God sent the Assyrian Army, a premier fighting force of the time, to conquer the northern kingdom, Israel, in 722 B.C., sending them into captivity. Later, Judah's southern kingdom was seized by the Babylonian Empire, which destroyed Jerusalem and sent the remaining Jews into exile in 587 B.C. God sent these national armies to defeat and discipline His people when they turned against Him. History has shown that every nation and empire have their beginnings, peak, and then fall. I pray that our country—the United States of America—

while having one of the world's best-equipped military forces, will always look to God as our major strength.

In the New Testament, we do not read much about military campaigns but how people serving in the Roman Army should act or behave toward others. In Luke chapter three, John the Baptist taught individuals and various groups of people who came to him asking what they should do to live better lives and be close to God. Verse 14 says, "Then some soldiers asked him, 'And what should we do?' He replied, 'Don't extort money and don't accuse people falsely—be content with your pay'" (NIV). John did not tell them to stop being soldiers; instead, they were to treat civilians around them with compassion, not abuse them, and be satisfied with their paycheck.

Armies have been notorious for pillaging and destroying farms, houses, cities, raping women, and mass murder. In the 1200s, when the Mongols were building and expanding their empire, they devastated many towns, killing millions of people and leaving piles of corpses. Their empire lasted over a hundred years, but they were eventually conquered and defeated.

Jesus had several encounters with Roman soldiers. In Luke 7:2ff, we read of a military officer who had a valued servant who was sick and near death. This centurion (a commander of *centuria*, meaning one

hundred, "the smallest unit of a Roman legion" [4]) sent some men to Jesus to ask for healing. He had enough faith for God's Son to say the word that healed his servant; Jesus commended him for his faith and healed his servant immediately. Jesus did not instruct soldiers they could no longer serve in the military but to obey the law and not mistreat people.

In the epistles or letters of the New Testament, both Paul and Peter showed knowledge of military matters and how soldiers should think and react. In this book, *Spiritual Battle Rattle: God's Armor*, and particularly this chapter, Paul writes: "Be strong in the Lord, and in the power of His might" (Ephesians 6:10, KJV). In the following verses, Paul tells us to put on or don the whole armor of God and describes the portions of spiritual battle gear to use and why we should use them. No doubt Paul came across many Roman soldiers during his multiple missionary trips and had a healthy respect for them. He was probably thinking about them when writing how we ought to be like soldiers in God's Army. In 2 Timothy 2:3-4, Paul addressed the young preacher, Timothy, in his last dispatch before death: "Join with me in suffering, like a good soldier of Christ Jesus. No one serving as a soldier gets entangled in civilian affairs, but rather tries to please his commanding officer" (NIV). A soldier back then (or any time) would always strive to be ready to march and fight the enemy. I cannot imagine a situation

where a Roman soldier would have a part-time or side job and prioritize that work over his military obligations. If foreign aggressors attacked the army, he might refuse his military duties because of his other job or life situations.

While in the Air Force, I had to report for work at various times of the day and night. I recall helping load cargo aircraft from our base before Operation Desert Shield in Iraq; when called to work, we were required to be there ASAP—no excuses. The apostle Peter wrote, "Be alert and of sober mind. Your enemy the devil prowls around like a roaring lion looking for someone to devour" (1 Peter 5:8, NIV). This verse lets us know who our enemy is. All military forces, especially commanding generals, seek to understand who they are fighting against and plan how to defeat them.

I like to read about the U.S. Civil War (or The War Between the States) and how the general officers fought against one another using tactics, weapons, and strategies. Most of them graduated from West Point and spent the early part of their adult life learning to be soldiers, and many deep, long-lasting friendships (and enemies) started there. They not only studied together, but they also fought in various wars together (e.g., Mexican and Indian Wars) and were knowledgeable about each other's strengths and weaknesses when the Civil War began. They were thus well familiar with each other, what they trained

to do, and would make battle plans accordingly. Stonewall Jackson was one of the south's greatest generals and won many victories. One of his greatest battles was in the Valley Campaign of 1862; with an army of around 17,000 men, Jackson defeated larger armies by using intelligence, boldness, and knowledge of his opponents.

In contrast to General Thomas Jonathan "Stonewall" Jackson (1824-1863) is General John Bell Hood (1831-1879). Many generals on the Union side knew that Hood was a talented fighter; however, he was not one of the smartest commanders. They used that knowledge to entice him to come out and fight. In 1864, Confederate General Hood temporarily took over Tennessee's Army from General Joseph Johnston. According to Wikipedia,

> Hood had a reputation for bravery and aggressiveness that sometimes bordered on recklessness. Arguably one of the brigade and division commanders in the CSA [Confederate States of America], Hood gradually became increasingly ineffective as he was promoted to lead larger, independent commands late in the war; his career and reputation were marred by his decisive defeats leading an army in the Atlanta Campaign and the Franklin-Nashville Campaign. [5]

At age 33, General Hood was one of the youngest men on either side of the Civil War to command an army.

By adopting a more army-like attitude in our spiritual lives, we will have a better opportunity for success against the devil and inferior forces. When a person first enlists in the U.S. military, they spend time in boot camp or basic training. In this setting, both men and women leave civilian life and mindset and train their bodies and minds to be more challenging, to put their desires aside, and work as a disciplined team to accomplish the mission, whether small or large. Trainees spend many months enduring countless physical and mental exercises to make them more challenging and protect themselves and their comrades.

As Christians today, we can use similar techniques or methods that soldiers, sailors, airmen, Marines, coastguardsmen, or guardians to help develop our spiritual lives. As men and women of faith, we need to build and deepen our relationship with God. One way is fostering a steady prayer life with Him. It is essential for us to communicate with God, to tell Him our needs, pains, concerns, and express our thanks for His blessings or gifts, whether physical or spiritual. Just as vital is developing a regular habit of reading the Bible and learning how God wants us to live.

In the Air Force, we had guidebooks called "Tech Orders." Every order would tell us what we needed to know, i.e., how to dress in our uniforms, how to perform our job (in detail), and so forth. You had to

follow the T.O.s, or else you could not complete your military job effectively or safely. During wartime, soldiers develop friendships and relationships to help them cope with various trials and battles they endured together.

As Christian brothers and sisters, our ability to develop and strengthen close relationships can make or break our ability to stay faithful. It helps us realize that while we are individuals and have a personal relationship with God, we are part of a more prominent family, a more significant force or army. We face an enemy who wants nothing more than separating us and picking us off one by one. By being together and strengthening one another, we raise individual and group success chances. We have a personal relationship with God, a relationship with close friends in the church, one with our local congregation, and one with believers worldwide. As many of us who have either served in the military or were military dependents or family members (i.e., military brat), there is nothing like the special relationship you develop in a congregation on or near military bases. There is a closeness that you cannot experience anywhere else.

The remaining chapters in this handbook will develop ways to strengthen our armor to defend ourselves—and our families—to defeat our common enemy. We all have unique skills and talents that are all necessary for the greater good. Remember the ending to the

song I quoted earlier? "… I'm in the Lord's Army! Yes, Sir!" The battle indeed belongs to the Lord (Proverbs 21:31). God's Army—*Strong*! ~ *JB*

Ed Linebaugh

U.S. Army, Retired

Email: more@minister.com

Joe Bryant

U.S. Air Force, Veteran

Email: joeauburn@att.net

CHAPTER TWO

ARMOR-UP

"Put on the full armor of God, so that you will be able to stand firm against the schemes of the devil … Therefore, take up the full armor of God, so that you will be able to resist on the evil day, and having done everything, to stand firm." (Ephesian 6:11, 13. All Scriptures are from the English Standard Version unless otherwise noted.)

———————————

The term so often used by people when faced with a problem is, "I've got this." Perhaps on most occasions, we do have it under control; however, we have not yet met all possible applications of life problems. When we think we have something under our control, we get hit in a direction from which we are unprepared. Sometimes, we do not even see it coming. What we face coming directly at us often looks much different when it is coming at us through someone we care for and love.

It was easy for me to philosophize about the death of a loved one before it touched my life in such a personal way. Losing my son and then my wife at thirty-nine years of marriage differed significantly from facing death myself. I remember thoughts of "Why did it happen like this?" "Why did the all-powerful God not intervene to keep this from

happening?" "A child is not supposed to die before his parents." While my wife lay in her casket, I asked myself, "Why can't I crawl in and be buried with her?" That choice was not mine to make—it was my task to face life head-on.

For those reading this chapter, you might face similar life tasks, regardless of what life is throwing at you. Our adversary, the devil, is looking for those "he may devour." He will look for different ways to approach the same problems, weaknesses, and sorrows. The only way to survive these difficulties is to "be strong in the Lord and in the strength [i.e., power] of His might." The victory is in Jesus, in the power of His might. The minute you think, "I've got this," you have lost the battle.

It is an honor to present this segment about "standing firm" in the whole armor of God as described in Ephesians six, verses eleven and thirteen. To address this subject adequately, I will touch on the various forms of armor discussed within the chapter, but I will try to "go easy" on what might be the subject in subsequent chapters of this book.

In Ephesians 6:10-13, the apostle Paul says:

> Finally, be strong in the Lord and in the strength of his might. Put on the whole armor of God, that you may be able to stand against the schemes of the devil. For we do not wrestle against flesh and blood, but against the rulers, against the

authorities, against the cosmic powers over this present darkness, against the spiritual forces of evil in the heavenly places. Therefore, take up the whole armor of God that you may be able to withstand in the evil day, and having done all, to stand firm.

These passages clarify the Devil is a schemer, a conspirator, a plotter. He will use whatever is within his arsenal and has no inhibition against coming at you through someone else. Verse 12, quoted above, speaks of who and where our fight lies. The idea of a physical flesh and blood fight is easy enough to understand, but what about the spiritual battle mentioned here? Are we going to fight in heaven or some Cosmic Battlefield? What does this mean?

I do not have all the answers to what all this means, but this much I know: we are informed this is our battlefield, so it is something that we are in contact with, and it is a war that we can fight. Not only can we *fight* in this conflict, but we must *also* win. The phrase, "against the rulers, against the authorities, against the cosmic powers over this present darkness, against the spiritual forces of evil in the heavenly places," does not imply leaders on the national scheme. It was written to speak of the ones with the rule and authority of darkness or sin and death. Furthermore, these rulers and leaders plan to bring things of the heavenly realm under their control, and we must fight against that.

Where exactly can we find heavenly places that we can influence? Is there such a thing or location where the battle is unseen from the standpoint of visual damage? If you are a Christian, do Christ and the Holy Spirit abide in you? What is the realm of Christ? Is it not a heavenly place? If He is in you, is not defending your soul a spiritual battle? What about your loved ones, family, friends, and the church? Are they worth fighting for? If so, you need to armor-up because the fight is already upon you.

It is often the item we fail to pack that we need the most. The thing we least expected is the very thing that happened. Murphy's Law idiom says, "whatever can go wrong will." Part two of this principle implies that when something goes wrong, it will generally occur in such a way as to be most disastrous. We all have vulnerabilities, and when the stakes are high, it is no time to "play it by ear." Remember the following phrases:

"A chain is only as strong as its weakest link."

"The Spirit is willing, but the flesh is weak."

"In a weak moment—let my guard down."

"Ill-prepared."

"Achilles heel."

SPIRITUAL

BATTLE   BATTLE

Wisdom from above (James 3:17) is the answer: God's Word as given in our Bibles. His Word may not provide a tailored response to your specific problem, but it presents guiding instruction or principles to apply to the correct course of action. In Ephesians chapter six, the point is exact: leave nothing unprotected; use the whole armor of God. Living a godly life and helping others to do so is not a spectator sport. We are on the battlefield and in the arena.

In this chapter, I will address the elements of Ephesians chapter six, verses eleven and thirteen. The most common focus of these Bible passages is the requirement to don the whole armor of God, and indeed, that is essential to engage in the battles we face successfully. This spiritual armor provides those things that protect our weaknesses and gives us the ability to fight the good fight of faith. As stated in verse eleven, God's battle array provides the things necessary to enable us to fight and win. His armor is not something that works without us but equips the soldier of Christ to be effective in battle. There are other elements in these passages that are rarely mentioned, such as the "Devil's schemes" and the "evil day." The term "do it all" implies leaving nothing undone. Of course, the term "stand" is vital. If one does not take a stand or position, nothing else matters. I would be remiss if I failed to address the necessity of standing firm.

Within the religious (i.e., Christian) world, a lot of talk focuses on the Battle of Armageddon in the Bible. This discussion centers on various theories and doctrines derived from a few verses in Revelation; however, the word "Armageddon" only appears one time (Revelation 16:16). Some contend that specific passages, such as Daniel chapter eleven, also address this conflict. The events described in Revelation address God's victory over Satan. It is senseless to discuss a global fight concerning Ephesians six, for, within this chapter, it is an *individual* battle and one that we each must fight. The apostle Paul points out that we are engaged in a spiritual struggle and warns that we must do all we can to be ready for the fight ahead. If we are unprepared, the action or battle will flow past us, and we will become one of its casualties. The word "stand" is defined as a *verb*, (1) "have or maintain an upright position, supported by one's feet," (2) "of an object, building, or settlement, be situated in a particular place or position." As a *noun*, (1) it is "an attitude toward a particular issue; a position taken in an argument," (2) "a rack, base, or piece of furniture for holding, supporting, or displaying something." [1]

More appropriately, as used in the above scripture, taking a "stand" is a determination not to be moved from a particular position, regardless of what comes your way. This determination or resolve has served well in establishing and preserving the freedoms we hold dear

in the United States. The Declaration of Independence serves as the foundation document for our rights and liberties; it lays out a firm belief in individuals' unalienable rights, and a determination to stand for those rights. It also notes that the stand we take has a price, a cost associated with that position. The last statement in this declaration includes the phrase, "we mutually pledge to each other our lives, our fortunes, and our sacred honor." Benjamin Franklin noted, "We must, indeed, all hang together or, most assuredly, we shall all hang separately." [2]

Failure to stand amounts to giving up on ourselves and the ones we love. It is contrary to God's will that any should perish (2 Peter 3:9). Our soul was important enough to God that He did not hold back His Son (John 3:16). Jesus dedicated Himself to the point of dying a miserable death (Philippians 2:8), and if our Lord did not give up on us, why should we give up on ourselves and those we love? Ephesians 6:10 reminds us to "be strong in the Lord and in the strength of His might." That is always the right place to start.

We will not always know the direction or nature of Satan's attacks. 1 Peter 5:8 describes our adversary as a "roaring lion, seeking anyone that he can devour." Although our spiritual fight's nature is addressed in another chapter, it is necessary to say a few words about it to understand what we are up against. Ephesians 6:12 reads, "For we do

not wrestle against flesh and blood, but against the rulers, against the authorities, against the cosmic powers over this present darkness, against the spiritual forces of evil in the heavenly places." It would be simple to identify a flesh and blood enemy, but that is not what we are dealing with here. Our struggle involves those who have control of situations much above our level. "In heavenly places"? It all sounds out of my league until I realize that the hearts and souls of God's people are a heavenly place. The New Testament speaks of the Lord dwelling within each Christian. In that sense, we are in a battle for our souls, the souls of our families, our homes, our neighborhoods, and everything affecting our eternal destination. Christians are under attack for our stand on life's sanctity and moral values. Society makes it appear as though Christians are the villains; we are under attack through the government legislature. Our children are under attack through their friends and the public education system. Our fight is real. The battle is not "over there somewhere" but is on the doorstep of our hearts and homes.

In November 2019, I presided over a wedding in Wales. During my travel from Brandon, Suffolk, England, where I worked with a military congregation, I encountered three different but somewhat related philosophies. (I presented all three as an appeal from my reasoning power as an intelligent human being.) My *first* contact occurred the day

before the wedding when I was at the Castle Coffee Shop in Cardiff, the capital city. A gentleman sat with me and brought up the question, "How can God be three persons (Father, Son, and Holy Spirit) and still be just one God?" I will not go into my response here, but I answered the question to the best of my ability, and the man left. My *second* contact occurred the evening after the wedding. I sat with an elderly guest, a gentleman in his nineties, who had served his church many years, and a young man who was dating the man's granddaughter. They held the philosophy that whatever we chose to believe would be okay in the eyes of God. It reminded me of the term in the Bible that each person "did what was right in his own eyes" (Judges 17:11). This gentleman also questioned the Scriptures' divinity (my thoughts associated with this discussion exceed this chapter). My *third* contact occurred after I caught the train back to England. My seat faced a table in the railcar, and a man was sitting across from me reading a book entitled "Unbelievable" by John Shelby Spong, a retired bishop of the Episcopal Church. Mr. Spong does not consider any of the Bible worthy of belief. For instance, he does not believe the creation story or any of the Old Testament's miracles; he also denies the divinity of Christ. The book questions everything about the Bible and says they are myths. You name it, and this gentleman sitting across from me gave Spong more credit than he did God and called himself

a "non-conformist." I could see the validity of that title. His sole argument was, "I don't believe it happened."

All three of the previous conversations occurred over four days. In every discussion, the person speaking to me approached their thoughts as an intelligent way to look at God and the Bible. Though I feel that I successfully addressed each situation, I felt like I was under attack when the third one was over, and many thoughts went through my mind. My strength indeed came from the Lord and the power of His might. Jesus said, "I am the vine; you are the branches … apart from Me, you can do nothing" (John 15:5). Many people get sucked in by worldly wisdom, which is "earthly, unspiritual, demonic" (James 3:15). Our enemy is powerful, but "the weapons of our warfare are not of the flesh but have divine power to destroy strongholds" (2 Corinthians 10:4). Remember, "he who is in you is greater than he who is in the world [meaning Satan]" (1 John 4:4). We take our stand in the Lord and the power of His might.

I thought about listing the enemy's weapons, but they are too many to mention here. The Apostle Paul told the Romans that the gospel is God's power unto salvation (Romans 1:16). He reminded the Corinthians that our stand is in that same gospel message (1 Corinthians 15:1). Paul also told the church at Philippi to stand firm in the Lord (Philippians 4:1). It is natural to feel that we are not adequate

for the task, and the apostle Paul felt the same way, so why should we think differently about our situation? The Lord's answer to Paul, and us, is simply, "My grace is sufficient for you, for my power is made perfect in weakness" (2 Corinthians 12:9).

There are three kinds of *rights*: (1) whatever is right in our own eyes, (2) whatever is morally right in the eyes of men, and (3) whatever is right in the sight of God. We must choose, and we must stand with what we desire. Rights or privileges are not tomorrow's fight; they are upon us right now, and we cannot afford to put it off as many important things are at stake. Therefore, one must be equipped with the *whole* armor of God, as our enemy knows our unprotected areas and incomplete armor. With all that God has given us, we can stand, but it takes His entire armor to succeed.

One other thing is yet lacking. Preparing ourselves with all the right weapons will do no good if, when the time comes, we cannot take a stand or position. The enemy is there; the battle is there, but the question is, are you in the fight? Do not concern yourself with the outcome. With God on our side, we cannot lose! Paul writes in Romans 8:35-39,

> Who shall separate us from the love of Christ? Shall tribulation, or distress, or persecution, or famine, or nakedness, or danger, or sword? As it is written, 'For your sake we are being killed all

29

the day long; we are regarded as sheep to be slaughtered.' No, in all these things we are more than conquerors through him who loved us. For I am sure that neither death nor life, nor angels nor rulers, nor things present nor things to come, nor powers, nor height nor depth, nor anything else in all creation, will be able to separate us from the love of God in Christ Jesus our Lord.

The writer of the book of Jude left the following words of encouragement in verses 24-25, "Now unto him that is able to keep you from falling, and to present you faultless before the presence of his glory with exceeding joy, to the only wise God our Savior, be glory and majesty, dominion and power, both now and ever. Amen" (KJV).

Now a few words about our fight or battle itself. As a former Marine infantry officer, I received training in war principles. We trained in methods to analyze potential threats and vulnerabilities, assess the enemy and his strengths, avenues of approach and venues of defense, and security to go on the assault or offensive. We regarded some places as more secure than others, but we knew each location has its vulnerabilities. To be an effective warfighter, the soldier must understand his goals and objectives. Preparing for spiritual battle, Christians must also have a clear picture of what they hope to accomplish. Who is your enemy? What are his objectives or goals? What does he hope to achieve, and how will he attempt to gain it? We

know he will try to trick and trap us, so what are our defenses against his treachery and snares or traps? Do not be ignorant of his methods but "be as wise as serpents, but harmless as doves" (Matthew 10:16). For what should we be ready? We learned that various "immediate actions" must be taken across multiple battle events during our training. For instance, when our patrol walked into "a kill zone" and attacked, our standard was to face our attackers and fight through them. It is tough, but you either do, or you die.

External events affect our fight, and we are often not in control. We control the action we take when faced with our enemy. Time is of the essence. When we reach a point where events have overcome us, we have already missed a critical opportunity. Every battlefield has conditions outside our control, but we cannot allow these conditions to rule the day. We have all the right tools, the correct armor to engage the enemy and win the fight. Sometimes we will come through with wounds and scars, but that does not mean that we have lost the battle. There is a "Balm in Gilead" to quote a hymn's name. Our Lord will provide our healing. We also need not think that we are alone in the fight. Our Christian brothers and sisters worldwide are engaged in similar battles, and our Lord, the Captain of our salvation (Hebrews 2:10), is with us.

Winning a war requires offensive action. A Prussian general named Carl von Clausewitz developed a stratagem entitled "The Principles of War." [3] Those same principles have been modified and are still taught in military colleges worldwide. Among the principles described are some that are useful in our spiritual battle. Essentially, von Clausewitz says to use what you have in the most effective way you can: use all the armor and bring that power to bear on the enemy. As Christian soldiers, we will only win if we are strong in the Lord and the power of His might, using the equipment that He has provided for our fight. Make your moves count as there is no time for trial and error. Exploit your successes and recover quickly from your mistakes because the second strike is coming. You cannot afford to be caught up in what you did wrong before and get broadsided because your brain seized up when you failed. There is also a principle called the "unity of command." For the Christian, there should be no question who our Commander is. We have His orders and His armor, so we are truly equipped for the fight.

As we close, let us look at the "evil day." What will it resemble? Will we see Satan coming with his legions to attack us personally, or will it be those troubles we face in the home, our family, our children, or our marriage? Will it be our children's problems from peer pressure, bullying, or will they need to conform to social pressures? Will they

come from the professional or job realm? Will they be things that attack the church, our brethren, our church leadership? The answer to these questions is yes. If you are single, Satan will seek to exploit your weaknesses and use various temptations, too many to mention here. All we can do is to put on and wear the whole armor of God and prepare for the fight as the scripture says, "that you may be able to withstand in the evil day, and having done all, to stand firm" (Ephesians 6:13).

Clif Hinds

U.S. Marine Corps, Veteran /

Department of Army Civilian, Retired

Email: hindsclif@yahoo.com

CHAPTER THREE

MILITARY INTELLIGENCE

"For our struggle is not against flesh and blood, but against the rulers, against the powers, against the world forces of this darkness, against the spiritual forces of wickedness in the heavenly places." (Ephesians 6:12. All Scriptures hereafter are as noted).

Since the Vietnam War in the 1960s and 1970s, and more recently in counterterrorism operations (i.e. Global War on Terror), NATO peace-support operation in Kosovo, Operations Enduring Freedom and New Dawn (Afghanistan and Iraq), the enemy was–and still is–difficult to detect as combatants and civilians are dressed alike and blend effortlessly into the surrounding culture. During previous theaters of operation like World War Two and Korea, each side in the warzone wore distinguishing uniforms to identify friend from foe with well-defined battle lines. Today's adversaries of our country have no such ready means of detection or territory.

The mission of military intelligence (intel) is to assemble and analyze as much data as possible to determine: (1) who the enemy is, (2) where the enemy is located and potential battlespace, (3) what the

enemy's tactics and weapon systems are, and how best to neutralize the enemy threat. "Duties of military intelligence specialists include conducting studies of missile sites and bases, foreign troop movement, and intercept foreign military conversation. They also spearhead investigation to neutralize national security threats." [1]

Military intelligence or MI has been around for centuries; in fact, it "is as old as warfare itself." [2] In the Old Testament book of Numbers, God ordered Moses to send out tribal leaders to explore the land He was giving to Israel (Numbers 13:2). These "intelligence agents" or spies were commanded to "see what the land [was], and whether the people who dwell in it are strong or weak, whether they are few or many, and whether the land that they dwell in is good or bad, and whether the cities that they dwell in are camps or strongholds, and whether the land is rich or poor, and whether there are trees in it or not" (Numbers 13:18-20, ESV).

According to Commander Bruce W. Watson, U.S. Navy Retired, Adjunct Professor of Soviet Studies, Defense Intelligence College in Washington, D.C., having reliable information could have averted the assault on Pearl Harbor that destroyed the U.S. Pacific Fleet and thrusting the U.S. into WWII. Commander Watson further states:

Today, nations have at their disposal information collection and processing systems that permit gathering and producing

intelligence more rapidly and more accurately than ever before. Satellites, ultramodern aircraft, electronic systems, human sources, cameras, imaging and electronic devices, and a host of other systems permit the amassing of information on a scale that was unheard of in the past. [3]

Just as U.S. military intelligence groups employ information evaluation tools around the world to gauge the enemy, so Christian believers must know and use all available spiritual intelligence to accurately assess and counterattack our common adversary. Mark Kelly, a former U.S. Army tactical intelligence officer, says that "in preparation for any battle the battlefield will always be analyzed. This is done to provide a combat force with the best opportunity for success." [4] Moreover, Kelly asserts:

> Failure to analyze the battlefield terrain will impede a commander from successfully maneuvering his forces. It reduces the chance for mission success and could very well cost the lives of his soldiers. What this means for the Christian warrior is that if you are not aware of the ways in which Satan can infiltrate your area of operation (where you live, work and play) then you cannot prepare a defensive strategy that will repel his attacks. He will then attack you in mass or stealthily penetrate the area in which you live from multiple directions. [5]

The U.S. Defense Intelligence Agency (DIA) falls under the overarching umbrella of the United States Intelligence Community, which is …

The nation's premier all-source military intelligence organization. It provides the nation's most authoritative assessments of foreign military intentions and capabilities. The agency's four core competencies – human intelligence, all-source analysis, counterintelligence and technical intelligence – enable military operations while also informing policy-makers at the defense and national levels. DIA's mission is unique and no other agency matches its military expertise across such a broad range of intelligence disciplines. [6]

According to DIA's official website, there are sixteen current members of the U.S. intel community (and the newly appointed U.S. Space Force Intelligence, Surveillance and Reconnaissance Enterprise) led by the Director of National Intelligence ranging from the recognizable Central Intelligence Agency, Federal Bureau of Investigation, Defense Intelligence Agency, and National Security Agency to lesser-known departments like the National Geospatial-Intelligence Agency and National Reconnaissance Office. [7]

So then, *who* is our real spiritual enemy? In what battlespace are he and his evil emissaries located? What are his weapons and tactics? How can we defend ourselves and neutralize our enemy before he wounds

or destroys us? We need information! We need intelligence! Like spiritual intelligence, spiritual mapping "is like reconnaissance … 'an inspection of a region to examine its terrain or determine the disposition of military forces.' We are in God's army and are engaged in a spiritual battle … if we are going to succeed in winning … we need to know what we are up against." [8]

Like the SACEUR at SHAPE headquarters in Mons, Belgium (I was stationed there for three years in the early 1980s), the highest military authority in NATO, God is our Supreme Director of Spiritual Intelligence. He is *omniscient* or all-knowing (1 John 3:20), *omnipotent* or all-powerful (Ephesians 3:20), and is *omnipresent* or present everywhere at any given time (Psalm 139:7-12). God has also provided His armed forces with explicit tactical information regarding our spiritual adversary. He has given us the best battle gear from heaven's armory (frankly, it has never changed from the original design and will not deteriorate or fail, unlike earthly military equipment) to defend us and neutralize our spiritual opponents. No weapon system upgrade needed.

Who is Our Enemy?

Hence, what do the spiritual intel (intelligence) and sitreps (situation reports) from heaven and recon (reconnaissance) missions from earth

say about our enemy? God's word notifies His army that "our struggle is not against flesh and blood, but against the rulers, against the power, against the world forces of this darkness, against the spiritual forces of wickedness in the heavenly places (Ephesians 6:12). The word "struggle" springs from the Greek word, *palē*, which means "to sway; generally fight; a wrestling bout; hence, a struggle, a conflict." [9] This encounter is unlike any high school or college wrestling contest, nor is it akin to professional sporting entertainment like World Wrestling Entertainment Friday Night Smackdown. Our country's wars were not about Adolf Hitler, Saddam Hussein, Osama Bin Laden, or other high-value targets or terrorists (yes, Hitler was undeniably a terrorist). However, as we will see, they plotted and executed (figuratively and literally) their self-serving, malevolent schemes. Our spiritual military campaigns have serious implications far beyond this life. Our battles are "against" (e.g., toward or regarding) those whose agenda and tactics emerge from enemy headquarters.

We shall now consider other Greek terms in our passage to help pinpoint our foe's unseen forces with whom we regularly clash. *First*, our struggles are with "rulers" (*archē* or chief leaders; compare with "anarchy" or the absence of authority or leadership). [10] *Second*, our struggles are directed toward "powers" (*exousia*)—that is, leaders who exert their abilities and influence over others. [11] *Third*, our struggles are

aimed at "world forces of this darkness" (*kosmokratōr* and *skotos* meaning "lord, master, or prince of the world of ignorance, ungodliness, and immorality").[12] *Fourth, and finally*, our struggles are in opposition to "spiritual forces of wickedness in the heavenly places." The term "spiritual" comes from the root word, *pneuma*, meaning "air; the disposition or influence which fills and governs the soul of any one; the efficient source of any power, affection, emotion, desire, etc." [13] Likewise, "wickedness" (*ponēria*) means "depravity, malice, evil purposes and desires." [14]

Before his name changed to Satan, the devil was known as *Lucifer*, which means "shining one, morning star" before getting the colossal head (i.e., prideful) and rebelling against God. He and his dastardly demons were booted out of heaven into eternal punishment (Isaiah 14:20; 2 Peter 2:4; Jude 6). Satan is known as the "ruler of the kingdom of the air" (Ephesians 2:2), "ruler of this world" (John 12:31; 14:30; 16:11), "god of this world" (2 Corinthians 4:4), "power of darkness" (Colossians 1:13), and "angel of the abyss" (Revelation 9:11). Furthermore, "names for the Devil are numerous … Prince of Darkness, Beelzebub, Mephistopheles, Lord of Flies, the Antichrist, Father of Lies, Moloch or simply Satan" besides Lucifer. [15]

Contrary to human invention or imagination, the devil is *not* some repulsive or hideous creature dressed in a red suit with pointed ears,

40

horns, and a tail holding a pitchfork as depicted in various images (why a pitchfork anyway?). What does he look like then? Indeed, not as we picture him (though he probably likes it that way to misinform us). He and his evil minions conceal themselves behind the cloak of religious and moral living. Like those dressed for a costume party, these "angels of light" (as described in 2 Corinthians 11:14) try to conceal their actual identity; however, to the trained eye of seasoned Bible students, they can be identified for who they are: faux, fake, and false—evil, erroneous, and egocentric.

Do not be fooled into thinking that Satan is done with you once you become a Christian! He tried every trick in his dirty little black book to get Jesus to sin. Thankfully for you and me, the Righteous One did not fall victim to the Evil One's wicked ploys! The devil knows he cannot win, but that does not stop him from firing salvo after salvo from his missile silos or underground launch facilities, often right on target. Some of Satan's attributes include being like a "roaring lion seeking who he will devour" (1 Peter 5:8), "a murderer from the beginning … a liar and the father of lies" (John 8:44), and "the accuser of our brethren" (Revelation 2:10). The devil is an instigator (1 Chronicles 21:1), a con artist (2 Corinthians 11:3-4,13-15), and a "deceiver" (Revelation 12:19). In essence, Satan is worthless, ruthless, dangerous, and an all-around loser with a huge "L" on his unseen

forehead. Satan and his appalling allies will use anyone and anything to his atrocious advantage, including you and your loved ones.

Where is Our Enemy Located?

Where does this spiritual battle with satanic forces occur? Paul says, "in the heavenly places" (*epouranios*), i.e., the "universe or world; the aerial heavens or sky, the region where the clouds and the tempests gather, and where thunder and lightning are produced." [16] Not only does our spiritual combat zone or battlespace envelop us, but it also occurs within the hidden recesses of our hearts and minds. If you let him have free rein within you, you will bring him into your military quarters where he will undoubtedly affect your family: your wife, your husband, your sons, and your daughters. Working through you and against you, the devil will also adversely affect your military community, your on-base school, your housing area, your duty station, and your unit.

Like an enemy spotter in the mountains of Helmand Province in southern Afghanistan, the devil has you and your family in his sights and is cocked, locked, and ready to rock! His aim is not to maim, though he will do whatever he can to weaken and overrun your defenses. Satan is on a personal search-and-destroy mission to snuff out your life and soul that you and those you dearly love will spend

eternity in hell with him and his Evil Special Forces (see Matthew 25:41 and Revelation 21:8). If you give him an inch, Satan will always take a proverbial mile.

What Weapons and Tactics Does Our Enemy Use?

Behind every war and every battle is a strategist or tactician—a mastermind who conspires and calls the shots.[17] Satan is an evil mastermind who dreams and schemes to draft his operation methods to attack and annihilate us. He is sly, sneaky, and a schemer—a master of disguise. Guerilla fighting is a "form of irregular warfare in which small groups of combatants, such as paramilitary personnel, armed civilians, or irregulars, use military tactics including ambushes, sabotage, raids, petty warfare, hit-and-run tactics, and mobility to fight a larger and less-mobile traditional military."[18] These maneuvers were deployed during the American Civil War where most of the guerillas were called "bushwhackers," because of their "tendency to hide behind foliage and forest lines … [they] were un-uniformed civilian resisters, who had no affiliation with the Confederate army, and were a source of constant confusion for the Union army who had no way of distinguishing a peaceful Southern civilian from one who would attack them later."[19]

Like Navy SEALs (Sea Air and Land), Air Force Special Ops, Army Ranger and Special Forces (e.g., Green Beret) units who covertly come close to enemy shores under cover of darkness to conduct clandestine recon operations to subvert and seize the enemy, the Evil Special Forces or Operations teams invariably lead guerilla-style or irregular warfare. One tactical approach he uses is what I call *voluntary infiltration:* we allow him to penetrate our hearts' defenses by not safeguarding entrance. Satan was seeking to kill Jesus and knew that one of the original apostles, Judas Iscariot, had a greedy heart (Matthew 26:14-15). He thus betrayed Him for a measly thirty silver coins (about $197 today): "the chief priests and the scribes were seeking how they might put Him to death; for they were afraid of the people. And Satan entered into Judas who was called Iscariot, belonging to the number of the twelve" (Luke 22:2-3). Thus, Judas voluntarily allowed Satan to enter and assault his heart's battlespace.

Satan uses multiple SWAT maneuvers; however, we shall only review two of them within the confines of this chapter. As Imperial Tactical Commander of Evil Forces with countless boots on the ground (i.e., the world), the devil uses various *temptation* to ensnare us as he did in the Garden of Eden with the First Couple (Genesis 3:1-8). The apostle John reports that Satan, as ruler of "the world," uses a three-pronged approach to tempt and capture our hearts and minds.

He has (1) "a craving for physical pleasure, (2) a craving for everything we see, and (3) pride in our achievements and possessions. These are not from the Father, but are from this world" (1 John 2:16, NLT). Still, "we don't want Satan to win any victory here, and well we know his methods!" (2 Corinthians 2:11, Phillips). If you are not aware or do not understand his schemes, *now* is the time to find out, not when you are spiritually wounded, gasping for air and waiting for spiritual first aid.

The Army "uses smoke and obscurants to attack Threat reconnaissance, surveillance, and target acquisition (RTSA) efforts. It also uses smoke to protect the force and support tactical deception operations. By combining obscuration with maneuver you can protect your force and deny the Threat the ability to acquire and engage it."[20] Satan also uses a type of *smokescreen* to blind, conceal, and confuse Christians engaged in spiritual combat. The apostle Paul clearly states, "Satan, who is the god of this world, has *blinded* the minds of those who don't believe. They are unable to see the glorious light of the Good News. They don't understand this message about the glory of Christ, who is the exact likeness of God" (2 Corinthians 4:4, NLT, emphasis added, *el*).

The word for "blinded" is *tuphloó* that metaphorically means "to blunt the mental discernment, darken the mind" (cf. John 12:40; 1 John 2:11).[21] In discussing the authorities' unbelief characteristic

45

during Jesus' day (and people of nowadays), the apostle John quoted the Old Testament prophet, Isaiah. "He has blinded their eyes and hardened their hearts, so they can neither see with their eyes, nor understand with their hearts, nor turn—and I would heal them" regarding the good news of Jesus (John 12:40, NIV). The allusion is to the devil deploying a similar tactic the Army uses to blunt and blacken the minds of Christian soldiers to the truth of the gospel in setting humanity free from the slavery of sin.

There is just no excuse for ignorance, as our Supreme Director of Spiritual Intelligence (God) has furnished us with vital intel to analyze and afford proper guidance and direction. We cannot and must not let the Evil One gain the tactical advantage. The apostle Peter cautions us to "stay alert. The Devil is poised to pounce and would like nothing better than to catch you napping. Keep your guard up" (1 Peter 5:8, Message). God told Cain, following the first fratricide of his brother Abel, "If you do well, will you not be accepted? And if you do not do well, sin is crouching at the door. Its desire is contrary to you, but you must rule over it" (Genesis 4:7, ESV). Attention! Hello, is anyone in there? Are you giving thought to your soul right now as you read this?

Once in your heart, and if left unrestrained, Satan will seize your thoughts and dominate your mind, albeit artful or subtle at first. For example, he will tempt you to glimpse at a pretty, scantily clad girl or

woman on a television commercial, Facebook advertisement, or maybe at the beach (really, anywhere now). You may think to yourself, "Well, at least I did not *stare* or *lust* after her." So, how long was that glance? True, maybe you did not commit adultery with her in your heart (at least yet), but what about the following image, commercial, or Facebook ad? A little longer gaze or peep perhaps—but not "that long," you say. How long next time and the time after that? (I am speaking from actual personal experience here.) Like the words of the hymn or spiritual song, "I am resolved no longer to linger, charmed by the world's delights."

Our joint enemy is not only zeroed in on you, but he is also skulking in the shadows, ready to rout your family, including your children. Scary? Yep. Reality check.

Every Christian is responsible for the defense and security of his/her area of operation. If you are a parent, you are further responsible for your children's area of operation as well. You need to have a clear understanding of how Satan will attack you and your family. You need to identify what avenue of approaches are [in] your area of operation. Identify where you are most spiritually vulnerable and work to build your defense in this area. What is the key terrain [i.e., battlespace] in your area of operation? We need to know what our area of interest is and how it impacts our area of operation in the spiritual war. [22]

While he tempts us to err, "Satan cannot force us to sin. He cannot control the behaviors of a believer, but he can place thoughts into our minds and lead us into temptation as a powerful strategy to lure us into sin." [23] It has been said that the best offense is a *strong* defense. On the spiritual battlefield of human hearts and minds, Christian warfighters must deploy their defensive gear and their offensive weaponry (i.e., the sword of the spirit and prayer as discussed in subsequent chapters of this book).

In closing, the Bible contains more valuable, actionable information than mentioned in this spiritual military intelligence overview. Some of the devil's attacks seem like mere skirmishes, while other episodes are all-out war. The more we know and understand about him, the easier it will be to recognize Satan's tactics and prepare for the inevitable spiritual battle. As alluded to in the above quote, every Christian, military or not, must study their Bible to identify and decide how our spiritual enemy will attack him or her. Be prepared to deploy for *spiritual combat*—be *spiritually strong* and healthy. While the battle belongs to the Lord and assures us victory (Proverbs 21:31), we are active-duty soldiers in His Army with divine directives and equipment to fight our enemy. To savor the sweet smell of conquest, as in Victory in Europe (V-E) Day or Victory in Japan (V-J) Day ending World War Two, we

must don, drill, and deploy daily with God's complete armor or *spiritual battle rattle* to be formidable—God's Army Strong!

Ed Linebaugh

U.S. Army, Retired

Email: more@minister.com

CHAPTER FOUR

WEB GEAR

"Stand firm therefore, having belted your waist with truth." (Ephesians 6:14. All Scriptures are from the New American Standard Bible.)

As military members, we are well acquainted with the gear that comes with our chosen profession. Essential equipment issued to soldiers includes a *web belt* from which other items needed in battle are clipped or attached, including first aid and ammunition pouches, a canteen for water, entrenching tool, and so forth. [1] Many elements are job-specific, while others are universal. Just as the U.S. Armed Forces has gear for physical warfare, the Bible speaks about essential items needed for spiritual warfare.

If we are to be what God has called us to be, we must take up the whole armor of God. Paul uses a verb in the imperative to describe our duty. In Ephesians 6:11, Paul tells us to "put on the full armor of God." Later this same command is given in verse thirteen to "take up the full armor of God." Why so much emphasis on this spiritual gear? Paul reminds his readers, "so that you will be able to stand firm against the schemes of the devil" (Ephesians 6:11b).

Peter also reminds us in 1 Peter 5:8, "Be of sober spirit, be on the alert. Your adversary, the devil, prowls around like a roaring lion, seeking someone to devour." Similarly, we are warned here in verse twelve about the spiritual fight we must endure. The warfare we face is not one with which we are often familiar. Many serving in the military have extensive training in physical and mental combat. Nothing can prepare us for the opposition we will face when confronted with Satan and his forces. If we try to rely upon ourselves and our might to defeat this foe, we will always fail. Living the Christian life will be a struggle, but it is a battle we can overcome with God's help. The beauty of this section of Scripture is that we cannot only overcome the devil's influence, but we can resist and stand firm. Paul likewise states in Romans 8:37, "But in all these things we overwhelmingly conquer through Him who loved us." We will be victorious over evil only if we are armed with God's goodness.

In this chapter, I encourage you to consider the battle array God has provided to military men and women (and all Christians) to stand against evil. Ephesians 6:14-18 specifically lays out this protective equipment supplied to us. These are necessary and essential to our victory with Christ.

In describing the armor of God, the apostle Paul begins with a seemingly impotent element: the *belt*. Yet, many in the military

understand the importance of the web belt as it is the central piece of battle rattle or gear. When Paul penned Ephesians, the Roman uniform belt was just as essential for battle as the sword and shield. It was an item that held the armor together and in place. It provided a place for other battle gear and rations, plus a scabbard or sheath for the sword. [2] In Paul's listing of battle gear, the belt is number one and is not a mistake. Just as any soldier's web belt today is at the center of his physical wellbeing, so truth is to every spiritual warrior today. Veracity is critical to every piece of the Christian's armor that will follow. Unlike the shield (verse 16) and the sword (verse 17) that defends or attacks in one direction at any given time, the belt always encircles us. The truth must surround faithful children of God. Regarding this section, one author states:

> Truth is important in Ephesians. It is revealed in the gospel (1:13; 4:15), and believers must be truth-speaking people (4:24-25; 5:9). As we buckle on this piece of the Messiah's armor, we live in His truth and speak His truth, displaying the characteristics of our victorious King. Do not give the Devil a foothold by neglecting to be a person of truth in your language, behavior, and attitude. [3]

While many people clamor for numerous truths, Jesus states that there is only one truth. Furthermore, we find that truth in the word of God. Jesus later appeals to God the Father in prayer, "Sanctify them

in the truth; Your word is truth" (John 17:17). If we want to know the truth, that which will make us free (John 8:32), we must live by the word of God. Will we change our lives to be under God's truth (1 John 1:6)? Will we put on the belt of truth?

A builder does not construct a house beginning with the walls or roof; his crew lays the foundation first. There is an order or process that must be adhered to, to ensure success. Similarly, the *belt of truth* is essential in its placement, for all things that follow will flow from it. This strap was a critical element in the battle armor in ancient days. It not only held all the connecting armor in place, but it also secured the soldier's tunic he pulled up for battle. It was central to the ancient Roman warrior, just as truth must be to the Christian soldier today. Truth must be at our core. It must be what we seek and long to find. The battle array element is crucial because all the rest will fail without it. If we do not acknowledge that absolute truth exists, nothing else matters. Righteousness, peace, and salvation have no reference and hold no value. The other armor elements are only as strong as our emphasis and dedication to the absolute truth.

We are amid a prevailing culture that speaks against absolute truth. [4] In this view, truth is not singular but placed on a spectrum. Postmodernism holds that there is no absolute truth. If any truth exists, it depends on the circumstances. Celebrities often claim to speak

their version of the truth and encourage others to do the same. The problem with this idea is that truth is not specific to any individual to make it our own. Truth is absolute. It is unchangeable. It is a standard, or it is not the truth.

What happens when we abandon absolute truth? Is it possible to find my truth? Suppose we travel down this road. Where does it end? Do we continue to claim that everyone has a right to their version of the truth when children are molested? Do we reject the absolute truth when women are raped? What about murder, theft, and abuse?

When we give up truth, there no longer remains a standard. If we can discover or invent our version of truth, then there is no right or wrong. Someone's choice to molest, rape, or murder is their expression of their truth. They cannot be called wrong if there is no standard to compare their actions. Can you see where this skewed thinking leads? This position is untenable, weak, and flawed. However, if there is a constant, unchangeable, unmovable truth, there is a standard or criterion to be upheld. Whenever we claim something was good or bad, we are referencing this absolute moral truth. Pilate, a Roman public official in Jesus' day, once asked an important question, "What is truth?" (John 18:38). Perhaps that is the question you are asking right now. Pilate directed his question to Jesus, who identified Himself as

the truth (John 14:6). Jesus is our sole source for truth, which is singular and critical in understanding the nature of truth.

We might notice Paul's argument in Ephesians chapter four, where he calls for unity. How might we be united? It is under a single truth. He explains, "There is one body and one Spirit, just as also you were called in one hope of your calling; one Lord, one faith, one baptism, one God and Father of all who is over all and through all and in all" (Ephesians 4:4-6). Notice there is not a diversity of truths; there is but one. Later in this chapter, Paul expounds upon the source of truth. He contrasts the world with its passions, greed, and wickedness (verse 19) and points us to someone who encompassed all truth: Jesus. Look at Ephesians 4:20-21, "But you did not learn Christ in this way, if indeed you have heard Him and have been taught in Him, just as truth is in Jesus." Make no mistake about it: when we find Jesus, we see the single, unadulterated truth of God. Truth has its genesis, its origin in God. Just as much as God is love (1 John 4:8), God is truth. That truth took human form (e.g., Jesus) to live among humanity.

Jesus speaks to the matter of truth as well. In John chapter 14, He is comforting His disciples. There was an immense need for consolation at this time because Jesus has just told His closest followers that He was going away (John 13:33), and they are visibly upset by this news. Thomas speaks up: "How do we know the way?"

Jesus answers with such simplicity, "I am the way, and the truth, and the life; no one comes to the Father but through Me" (John 14:6). Talk about comfort! Jesus wanted His disciples (and us) not to be confused about which direction they should go. It would become more apparent as they followed Jesus and thus the truth.

But Jesus does not stop there as He explains the truth. Later in the same gospel account (John 17), He prays to God the Father. Jesus spoke of His purpose (verses 1-3), has asked for divine blessings upon the disciples (verses six and following), and requested that those who follow Him be set apart (i.e., made holy or consecrated). Therefore, Jesus prays, "Sanctify them in the truth; Your word is truth" (John 17:17). He told us precisely where we meet that truth: when we regard the word of God. That is the standard for truth—it is our measuring rod.

Just as Jesus had emphasized truth later in His ministry, He also spoke of it early in His earthly ministry. In some ways, John chapters thirteen and fourteen mirror John chapter eight. Here again, we see Jesus talking about going away. He proclaimed to the Jews who had believed in Him, "If you continue in My word, then you are truly disciples of Mine; and you will know the truth, and the truth will make you free" (John 8:31-32). Jesus does not mince words when He states the source of truth. His words are authentic and valid. That is

something no one can say today regarding their vocabularies. As students of God's word, we can be ambassadors or representatives of truth, but we will never be the source of that truth, for truth does not live within us.

As Jesus stood an innocent man in front of a raging mob who shouted for His death, Pilate, the Roman governor, pulled Jesus aside to speak candidly with Him. In Luke's gospel, Pilate had referred to Jesus as a king, and here in John, he further cross-examines Him. Jesus' response was clear: "You say correctly [truth] that I am a king. For this I have been born, and for this I have come into the world, to testify to the truth. Everyone who is of the truth hears My voice" (John 18:37b). Jesus is consistent in His teaching. Just as He had said this about Himself in John chapters 8, 14, and 17, He reiterates here that He is the source of all truth.

Jesus testified to absolute truth and the word of God. There is truth in its entirety, and it is only found in Jesus and His words. If we are looking for a pattern of truth, look no further than Christ. Truth is the battleground upon which we are fighting. On one side is Christ, our Redeemer who is perfect truth, and on the other side is Satan, who perverts truth. To put our faith, hope, or trust anywhere else is futile, a waste of time. We must act decisively with Christ and the armament

SPIRITUAL
BATTLE BATTLE

He provides. We dare not search anywhere else for a benchmark of truth as there is no other.

Just as Paul stated at the beginning of his listing of battle armor, truth must be foundational to our lives and faith. That means that Jesus must be at the center of our lives. He is our source for truth, our standard. The apostle John further spoke to this fact:

> You are of your father the devil, and you want to do the desires of your father. He was a murderer from the beginning and does not stand in the truth because there is no truth in him. Whenever he speaks a lie, he speaks from his own nature, for he is a liar and the father of lies. But because I speak the truth, you do not believe Me. (John 8:44–45)

Jesus makes a stark contrast here. As we have seen in the Bible, Jesus is the truth; that is, His ways and words are authentic. Yet, many oppose Him, and they are like the devil. I draw this parallel because, just like the devil, they do not stand in the truth. Jesus was telling the truth to the world, and they opposed the Son of God. They were not acting according to the truth.

We must be standing firm in the truth of God—His word anywhere else is a vicious battleground. This information implies that we must know the truth. We must live in the truth, and all truth must live in us. By understanding the truth, we will know what is false. We will be able

to identify the lies of the world because they will be visible in the light of the word of God. Knowing the truth will allow us to see our past mistakes to correct our future. Knowing the truth helps us to see the devil's lies. And like the ancient Roman warrior's web belt encompassing them, we must always be secured with the truth. Sadly, those who try to follow God and His word are labeled hateful and intolerant for holding to the standard of absolute truth. This fact has persisted through the centuries, and nothing has changed in that regard today.

How do those who hold to absolute truth move forward despite the constant pushback from a world that retains a comparative view of reality or truth? We must be consistent. As we review today's religious landscape surrounding us, notice the vast number of churches and an equal number of varying beliefs. If we uphold the view that there is an absolute truth, then we cannot say all this disparity is simultaneously the truth. If we adhere to a standard of verity, Jesus, and His words, we must take what He says to heart. We cannot merely go to any church and think we are okay because we then live a contradiction. There is no way to call all churches the same because they do not practice or teach the same things. Since we desire to follow the standard of truth, which is Jesus, we must examine these differences. We must worship where people follow the truth of God's word and

not just give lip service to it. It is of the utmost importance for every fabric aspect of our lives. We must worship and live the way God desires to please Him.

Jesus, in speaking to the crowd in His famous "Sermon on the Mount," teaches about adhering to the truth in Matthew 7:21-23,

> Not everyone who says to Me, 'Lord, Lord,' will enter the kingdom of heaven, but he who does the will of My Father who is in heaven will enter. Many will say to Me on that day, 'Lord, Lord, did we not prophesy in Your name, and in Your name cast out demons, and in Your name perform many miracles?' And then I will declare to them, 'I never knew you; depart from Me, you who practice lawlessness.'

Again, Jesus teaches that there is a standard, and we are not it. If we are not doing as God has asked of us, we will not live according to the truth. Jesus says we are workers of lawlessness if we do not adhere precisely to His teaching. Just as we must keep our focus fixed on truthfulness, we must also realize that we will never be the truth. At our best, we will be lights that shine brightly because of the light of the truth. We are only examples of what it looks like to follow the truth. Our cherished duty is to point others to Christ so that He might gain the glory and honor that is rightly due to Him. When we focus on truth, it has a way of reminding us of how insignificant we are, yet God

can use us for such grand means. He can enable us to be ambassadors of the truth, allowing us access to it far and wide.

In conclusion, as we remember our place in God's grandiose scheme of redemption, we should be amazed at His love. He sent His only Son, Jesus the Christ, to die for our sins. It is because of what He did on the cross to equip us with the *web belt of truth*. That is at our center and is a powerful reminder of who God is and who we are to Him. It likewise reminds us of the great blessing of truth that we have and in which we stand.

Freddie Klein

U.S. Air Force, Veteran

Email: fredrickklein00@gmail.com

CHAPTER FIVE

BOOTS ON THE GROUND

"Having strapped on your feet the preparation of the gospel of peace." (Ephesians 5:15. All Scriptures stated hereafter are from the New International Version)

Boots on the ground: what does this phrase mean? The late General Volney Warner coined this expression during the Iran Hostage Crisis in 1980. This quote from Wikipedia is helpful to understand this phrase:

> Warner is credited with coining the phrase 'boots on the ground', to mean the actual forces engaged in a conflict. The first use of the phrase is identified as a quote in the *Christian Science Monitor* (April 11, 1980) in reference to the Iran hostage crisis: 'U.S. options grow more difficults [*sic*] as the chance of a Soviet response increases. However, many American strategists now argue that even light, token U.S. land forces — 'getting U.S. combat boots on the ground' as General Warner puts it — would signal to an enemy that the U.S. is physically guarding the area and can only be dislodged at the risk of war. [1]

After our sins are washed away in baptism, I have heard the question asked, "Why does not God just take us straight to heaven?"

Because He has a mission for us here! We are here as His "boots on the ground." He wants the world's unbelieving population to know that He is concerned about them. Just as a new military officer receives their commission before starting their active-duty service, God has a commission for His people:

> Then Jesus came to them and said, 'All authority in heaven and on earth has been given to me. Therefore, go and make disciples of all nations, baptizing them in the name of the Father and of the Son and of the Holy Spirit, and teaching them to obey everything I have commanded you. And surely, I am with you always, to the very end of the age.' (Matthew 28:18-20)

The great Christian writer C. S. Lewis wrote, "Enemy-occupied territory – that is what the world is. Christianity is the story of how the rightful king has landed, you might say landed in disguise, and is calling us to take part in a great campaign of sabotage." [2]

"Boots on the ground" shows a commitment. During my Air Force service, I spent a tour in South Korea. Much further north on the Korean peninsula, the Army's Second Infantry Division was positioned to oppose any possible North Korean attack. Their nickname was "The Second Speed Bump." We all knew that many of their positions would be "speed bumps" to the enemy if there were a surprise attack. However, they would buy time for the rest of us to

mount a defense. All of us were part of a tripwire: if the North Koreans attacked us, we knew that a large contingent of our brothers and sisters from all branches of the U.S. military would soon be in-country to support us.

As God's "boots on the ground," we serve as His ambassadors. The apostle Paul notes that "we are therefore Christ's ambassadors, as though God were making his appeal through us. We implore you on Christ's behalf: Be reconciled to God" (2 Corinthians 5:20). Unbelievers do not understand that while they remain separated from God, they are His opponents: "For if, when we were God's enemies, we were reconciled to him through the death of his Son, how much more, having been reconciled, shall we be saved through his life" (Romans 5:10). As spiritual diplomats, God has committed us to a reconciliation or reunion ministry. Paul again points out in 2 Corinthians 5:18–19 that "all this is from God, who reconciled us to himself through Christ and gave us the ministry of reconciliation: that God was reconciling the world to himself in Christ, not counting men's sins against them. And he has committed to us the message of reconciliation."

God has positioned us in many locations to develop relationships with many different people in various life statuses. Some are single, and some have families. Some have brand new babies, and others are

SPIRITUAL
BATTLE BATTLE

empty nesters. Regardless of our situation, we need to remember Philippians 3:20a, "But our citizenship is in heaven." Our Leader (God) wants the size of His kingdom expanded.

As we interact with people, we must realize that we are in a spiritual struggle, a battle between good and evil. In Ephesians chapter six, Paul writes about the armor of God, something that only a soldier requires. Armor implies that there will be a conflict with someone intending to cause harm. A farmer does not need it to plant or harvest. A mechanic does not need it while repairing a piece of machinery. A teacher does not need it to teach history (on second thought, it might comfort some schools!). However, soldiers need their battle armor!

Just as we need to be actively involved in the battle, we need to encourage our brothers and sisters; many are content to sit back, rather than engage in the fight. Figuratively, they may want to stay in the barracks, not be on the battlefield. Sadly, they might display very few differences from non-Christians, such as using vulgar language or becoming easily angered. Christians in the military might also engage in mean, vengeful discourses on social media. Instead of growing in Christian qualities, they may become stagnant.

Years ago, while serving in the Air Force Reserve Officer Training Corps (ROTC), we studied leadership principles for armed forces

officers. I remember an example from the Army, which also applies to the church. The book presented a situation facing a brand-new Army infantry lieutenant taking his soldiers into combat for the first time. What should his first action be? Should he fire his weapon? Should he radio the command post that he is under fire? I found the suggested solution to be fascinating. Lieutenants must traverse up and down the line to ensure their men are fighting. Americans are not natural killers, so there may be a reluctance to use their weapons. The lieutenant firing his individual weapon is only one weapon. Ensuring that every soldier is engaged in fighting the enemy vastly increases the overall effect.

In church life, Americans are typically reluctant to engage the world with the Gospel's message. We need to encourage them and model ways of telling others about Christ. People will not always do things the way we think they should, but if they try to glorify God, help, and do not hinder them. Consider how Barnabas, the "Son of Encouragement," introduced Paul (Saul before his conversion) to the apostles: "But Barnabas took him and brought him to the apostles. He told them how Saul on his journey had seen the Lord and that the Lord had spoken to him, and how in Damascus he had preached fearlessly in the name of Jesus" (Acts 9:27). His introduction and support were foundational to Paul's ministry.

What Are Some Ways That We Can Use Our

Time Here to Glorify God?

RECRUITING: Additional "boots on the ground" need to be drafted or recruited (in Biblical terminology, this is *evangelizing*). Recruiting is a TOUGH job and requires a tremendous amount of perseverance. We need to pray that God will bring people into our path for us to tell them about the significant benefits of God's Army. As the adage goes, its retirement plan is out of this world.

TRAINING: To be better recruiters, we need instruction. We must learn new evangelistic techniques (without changing the gospel, of course) and adapt as the culture changes. We need lifelong training in discipleship; however, this is a two-way street. We not only need to be teaching others to enhance their walk or Christian lifestyle, but we must also learn from others and grow ourselves. There are two significant bodies of water in the Bible lands—the Sea of Galilee and the Dead Sea. The Sea of Galilee is where the apostles fished, and people still fish those waters today. In contrast, there are *zero* fish in the Dead Sea due to its salinity, which kills life; thus, it is the *Dead* Sea. However, water continuously flows in and out of the Galilean sea, keeping it refreshed, whereas water entering the Dead Sea stays there

and becomes stagnant. We need to be like the Sea of Galilee rather than the Dead Sea.

UNIT INTEGRATION (Fellowship): Just as a new trooper needs to meet people in their new unit and become a part of it, the new Christian needs to assimilate and meet his new family. They need to learn about one another. While they will receive support from other Christians, new converts will also need to support others (we called it fellowship, and it is vital). One thing I remember from my ROTC training long ago was the fact that soldiers will fight better as a team. If possible, you do not want just one person out in the foxhole but give them some support with a second person. When Jesus sent out the disciples, He sent them out in pairs, providing mutual aid. We need to look at this as our example, and not movie icons like John Wayne or Clint Eastwood who go it alone.

COMMUNICATION (Prayer): The new Christian soldier in God's Army must learn how to communicate on multiple levels. Most importantly, they must learn to speak with God. It is sometimes easy to do all the talking, but we also need to know how to listen. Like discipleship, communication is a two-way street.

LEGACY: Unit history has long been a part of military history. It is good to develop a "dual" vision if the new Christian creates a "dual"

concept. It is very instructive to look back at those who preceded them. Consider the brave martyrs and others (see Hebrews chapter eleven) who courageously stood for God against tremendous odds. Think forward: consider your legacy; how many people will be in heaven because of your efforts to follow God?

RULES OF ENGAGEMENT: How can we influence our culture? How we act/react is vital. There is so much venom in the world today. "Discussions" on social media often quickly devolve into name-calling and vicious attacks. "To slander no one, to be peaceable and considerate, and to show true humility toward all men" (Titus 3:2) should always be in the back of our minds when responding to comments. Another excellent verse is Romans 12:18, "If it is possible, as far as it depends on you, live at peace with everyone."

SERVICE OPPORTUNITIES AND SPECIALTIES: The military assigns codes to various job classifications: in the Army and Marine Corps, these codes are Military Occupational Specialty; in the Air Force, they are Air Force Specialty Codes; and the Navy classifies their jobs as "ratings." These are areas where personnel train and then use their education for the good of the service and the nation. The Bible lists out some specialties: "It was he who gave some to be apostles, some to be prophets, some to be evangelists, and some to be pastors

and teachers, to prepare God's people for works of service, so that the body of Christ may be built up" (Ephesians 4:11–12).

What Areas Can We Serve Today?

(Bias alert—my wife was a children's minister for years. She always wanted to get more men involved with the children). Let us men be *men* and consider helping our wives with the children! Today, many kids live in a single-parent home, usually a female who holds the family together. Typically, they do an excellent job in a difficult situation. However, the children need to see that both men and women are involved in the church. We do not want young boys to look at the church and think it is only for females. When I was a kid, my father seldom went to church, so I did not want to go either. Again, men need to be role models and magnify Jesus to the kids.

PRAYER: We cannot provide "air support" for each other as the Air Force does for the Army and Marines, but Christians can and must provide "prayer support." Pray for the unsaved. Pray for your preacher, elders, and deacons. Pray for wisdom (James 1:5) on how our lives can reflect Jesus. Consider going above and beyond and serve in your church's prayer ministry. Be a prayer warrior!

INVOLVEMENT: Be actively involved in discipleship. Look for people who are further along in their spiritual walk. Seek those who

are wise and willing to share that knowledge. Seek their counsel. Incorporate it into your life, and then find younger people you can mentor. (For the astute reader, you have noticed that I mentioned discipleship earlier. You might think I am old, senile, and forgetful. These are true to some degree, but I did it intentionally.) Repetition shows importance, and discipleship is essential. Please realize that God has given you unique gifts and talents. If you feel inclined to serve in a particular area, go for it, for the glory of God.

In closing, it is crucial that we, as "boots on the ground," are active as God's emissaries or ambassadors. When Christ comes again or when we breathe our last breath, let God find us busy glorifying Him. May He say to each of us on the Judgement Day, "Well done, good and faithful servant" (Matthew 25:23).

Steve Leaming

U.S. Air Force, Veteran

Email: sleaming51@gmail.com

CHAPTER SIX

MISSILE DEFENSE

"In addition to all, taking up the shield of faith with which you will be able to extinguish all the flaming arrows of the evil *one*." (Ephesians 6:16. Unless otherwise noted, all Scriptures in this chapter are from the New International Version)

Notice first, the inspired writer of Hebrews (whom many believe was the apostle Paul) rouses his readers to embrace a concept that is the basis of all Christianity, and our study in Ephesians six, that "without faith it is impossible to please God" (11:6).

Missile defense is a critical element of our nation's military, so I cannot help but think about the Air Defense Artillery at Fort Bliss, Texas. While stationed at William Beaumont Army Medical Center, adjacent to this artillery hub, I was privileged to speak with several soldiers directly involved with this military profession on many occasions. Air defense artillery was a primary mission then, as it remains today. There have been significant technological advances in this defense system vital to the welfare of the United States and its interests, just as the *shield of faith* is of primary importance to the

SPIRITUAL BATTLE BATTLE

Christian's welfare. But what does it mean to "take up the shield of faith"?

The shield is something that an ancient soldier carried to help guard the vital organs of his body, especially the heart. We may consider a modern soldier or law enforcement officer wearing a Kevlar vest for protection. We often think of security from a human physiological point of view because we understand the heart's function and the critical nature if it is damaged. However, the term "heart" is often used to describe an individual's psychological or spiritual state. So, the shield of faith is that implement or piece of armor that protects one from the flaming arrows or all those worldly thoughts and actions from the devil, which could damage our physical body, mental health, and spiritual well-being.

We are not the first, nor will we be the last, generation to struggle with the idea of faith in an omnipotent, omniscient, and omnipresent Being in our life. At Jesus' transfiguration, Peter, James, and John had finally grasped the truth about who Jesus was by the only means possible to learn the truth—through faith. [1] The apostles witnessed something that was truly beyond their comprehension, and it is recorded for us so that we too might come to the same realization: to have faith in Christ, His power, and the redemption of His life and

sacrifice. Faith dispels fear; it sets us free from the devil's schemes and fills us with joy and peace.

During my early growing years, one of my mentors used a saying that has stuck with me regarding one's conscience. If you were to force a square peg in its hole, then somehow begin to turn it with great force, eventually, you would make a round hole through which that square peg could now rotate freely. Our consciences operate similarly; if we violate our principles and continue to do so, ultimately, our conscience will become so callused that we would not be able to discern the difference between right or wrong. Therefore, we must protect all aspects of our hearts from the evil one to prevent us from a callused or hardened state of mind or body.

When I was preaching, I enjoyed using acronyms—words that meant something within the lesson that helped the listener remember the lesson's vital points (the military has a plethora of abbreviations for each branch of service). I will employ that exact principle in this chapter for the same reason, so I will use the first letter of the seven days of the week to fulfill this goal.

Taking up the shield of faith involves protecting every aspect of the Christian's life: heart, soul, conscience, and physical wellness. Doing so means we are to 'STUDY to shew thyself approved unto God, a

workman that needeth not to be ashamed, rightly dividing the word of truth" (2 Timothy 2:15, KJV). While this version uses the word "study," many others use "be diligent" or other words with a closely related meaning. While many of us probably take Bible study for granted on SUNDAYS, many may not have developed a routine for daily Bible study, so that dedication does not come naturally. Being diligent means that we must make a regular, conscious effort to make it a routine habit. Diligence is a trait of the ancient and modern soldier.

Being prepared mentally, physically, and for many, even spiritually, to combat the enemy takes effort and tenacity and, thus, an initial step of taking up the shield of faith. When I retired for the second time three years ago, one goal I set for myself was to make Bible study an integral part of my morning routine. So far, I have been successful in doing this, and I must admit that it has certainly helped me remain on the straight and narrow. That thirty minutes to an hour each day provides an enormous boost to my spiritual well-being and, I am convinced that it aided my mental and physical wellness. However, to be transparent, my time spent could be improved significantly, as I will explain shortly. On Sundays and daily throughout the week, being diligent in learning more about what God says in His holy Word, and exercising that knowledge by teaching and admonishing or warning (as needed), is one of the initial steps in taking up the shield of faith.

MONDAYS can present a real challenge to many people. The beginning of a new workweek can reveal new responsibilities, incite trials, test our resolve, and disrupt schedules. Another method of donning the shield of faith is to MEDITATE, which entails establishing a time of day that is quiet and secluded. Our time of meditation should involve prayer, a vital means of communication with God, our Heavenly Father, to express our praise, thanksgiving, petitions, contrition (repentance), or remorse over our sins. It might even include spending some time memorizing scripture. Nothing can better prepare us to meet daily trials and temptations than embedding the words found in the Bible in our minds.

Meditation is one of my weaknesses; I often get sidetracked during Bible study, thinking about the cares of the day, which hinders a meaningful time of reflection and prayer. My encouragement is this: do not get discouraged about the distractions and try harder to focus on our spiritual wellness and others. When praying for others, I have noticed that my praise and thanksgiving for my blessings are expressed more readily and earnestly. Besides those methods of meditation just mentioned, we can employ this vital step in taking up the shield of faith by thinking about or planning how we can be more valuable to the Lord in our daily walk. We will open ourselves to allow the Holy Spirit to lead us into greater spiritual growth levels during this process.

One of the closest related words to faith is TRUST. While commuting to work on TUESDAY, we trust that our vehicle will help us arrive on time and safely. We trust that fellow drivers on the roadways will obey the laws that keep us safe while traveling. Similarly (and hopefully), we trust God to provide peace, comfort, sustenance, and safety daily with a greater sense of respect. Not to be redundant, but we must also trust that He has provided us a place in the heavenly home and His Son's sacrifice that makes that possible. There is an old hymn that I have not heard sung in many years entitled *Trust and Obey*. Some of the lyrics can help us understand there is no other way to be happy in Jesus. If you are unfamiliar with the song, please look in most hymnals, note the lyrics, and make them a part of your thought process in preparing for a new day. Not only must we trust in Jesus, who is the only source of our spiritual salvation, but we must also trust each other to encourage us in that spiritual journey of being more Christ-like. Again, we should trust in the Bible's validity as God's inspired Word.

There is so much going on in our society today where people are doing their best to discredit the Bible, and it is essential that we maintain our trust in its truthfulness. "All scripture is God breathed and is useful for teaching, rebuking, correcting and training in righteousness" (2 Timothy 3:16). Taking up the shield of faith requires

a level of trust that this statement is not only factual but an essential component of our spiritual well-being.

The middle of the week, WEDNESDAY, requires a certain level of WORK to make it through our, western society-generated, "hump day." Most of us know that genuinely putting on the shield of faith takes work. Working in the hospital during my Army career, I never had to don Kevlar gear; however, I know it has been made relatively simple with little "work" of putting on a protective vest. However, donning the shield of faith is unlike most "work" we are familiar with.

The work of sharing the Good News of Jesus is of paramount importance to the Christian soldier. Romans 10 explicitly addresses the preacher of the Gospel; note Paul's words in verse 17, "Consequently, faith comes from hearing the message, and the message is heard through the word about Christ." The preacher's work helps people hear the message, and that work involves preparing it so that people understand it and that it applies to them personally. Before the above passage, Paul asks a series of questions: "How, then, can they call on the one they have not believed in? And how can they believe in the one of whom they have not heard? And how can they hear without someone preaching to them? And how can anyone preach unless they are sent? As it is written: 'How beautiful are the feet of those who bring

good news!'" (verses 14-15). Praising those who work to preach the gospel, as Paul does here, is a task that we all can accomplish.

Thus, this admonition and encouragement to work is a call for every Christian to realize and act upon that our very lives are to be witnesses of Jesus in everything we try to accomplish. We often pray that God will use us to be the hands and feet of Jesus in our daily lives. As I wrote this chapter in April 2020, we struggled with a "stay at home order" by the federal and state governments because of the novel (new) coronavirus or COVID-19. Every day, nearly everyone is working to maintain their health and sanity within their immediate family. Healthcare workers are overburdened, sometimes beyond their capabilities. I have worked in healthcare for most of my adult life; it is reasonably easy for me to understand the struggles they face daily, knowing they expose themselves to a potentially lethal virus. As Christians, we must act as spiritual healthcare givers in the sense that we should offer our "bodies as a living sacrifice" (Romans 12:1) to others to help them understand that life is short and can be taken away from us at a moment's notice. Therefore, we should labor daily, allowing our living habits and mannerisms to reveal our commitment to follow the example of Jesus as He exemplified God's Word. Consistent work of this nature is evidence of "taking up the shield of faith."

Since THURSDAY does not mark the end of the workweek, it remains a day to TRAVERSE or navigate the obstacles that may hinder our routes to productivity in our jobs, or more importantly, our paths towards righteousness. In Matthew chapter seven, Jesus warns us that the gate and road that leads to destruction are wide, while the gate and road that leads to life are narrow, and only a few will find it (verse 13). But He continues preaching about those false prophets that approach stealthily and calls them ferocious wolves and that their bad fruit will be recognized. We all can probably relate to and understand the perils of the devil. Many of us committed 1 Peter 5:8 to memory at an early age: "Be alert and of sober mind. Your enemy the devil prowls around like a roaring lion looking for someone to devour."

We must negotiate those obstacles in our personal lives that keep us from focusing our attention on Jesus. An air defense artilleryman must traverse some rugged and challenging terrain in Afghanistan to ensure his targeted objective is the only thing destroyed. I learned the term "traverse" while being trained in land navigation techniques. Later in my Army career, I discovered that a soldier might become disoriented when trying to cross various types of terrain instead of using the compass to keep on the direct path and navigate through terrain so that you arrive at the intended destination. The devil causes us to divert our attention on so many different issues in our daily lives,

trying to keep us from following that straight and narrow path that leads to eternal life. The apostle Paul provides us an excellent example when he exclaimed: "I press on toward the goal to win the prize for which God has called me heavenward in Christ Jesus" (Philippians 3:14). Let us traverse or navigate the obstacles that keep us from maintaining our focus on Jesus while using the Bible as our spiritual compass to do everything we can to remain on the path to life eternal, thereby taking up and using the shield of faith.

As FRIDAY rolls around, we might have to FIGHT through traffic to get home in time to prepare for the weekend of recreation and relaxing. Yes, we may have to show some offensive tactics at times to reveal our willingness to combat the devil's schemes (note that Jesus rebuked Peter for his lack of belief). You probably have heard the saying, "the best defense is a great offense." While the shield may be a defensive weapon, defense or security protects the vital functions described earlier. Fighting and resisting are synonymous when it comes to temptations. So, fight the temptation to be lazy on Sunday morning and not make it to Bible class or the worship service. Fight the anxiety and fear present in so many different situations. Fight the urge to lash out at the colleague who belittles you for no apparent reason. Fight the temptation to be afraid of speaking out against the sin that surrounds you. Many scenarios are illustrating this point. To take up the shield of

faith, one must be willing to battle against those forces which the evil one throws in our path daily.

SATURDAY ushers in new challenges where we need to SHOW our resolve to live the Christian life, as we promised ourselves to live daily for Lord. One of the best ways to show our love for God is to engage with Him in prayer. He continually shows His love for us as revealed in the first part of 1 John 3:1, "See what great love the Father has lavished on us, that we should be called children of God." Thus, we should reciprocate God's love by continuous communication with Him via prayer. There are countless ways to express our love for God and, consequently, demonstrate our love for others. Note these three examples: (1) use your influence to invite your friends, family, or neighbors to worship; (2) volunteer for the neighborhood food distribution to the needy; and (3) send encouraging messages to those of whom who are sick and in need, bereaving, or lonely. Of course, there are innumerable other ways to prove the love of God to others. Through any of these or other different ways, we are not only showing our love for Him but performing a necessary step to take up the shield of faith.

In summary, I believe the following tips will help us take up and use the shield of faith by considering the seven days of the week. STUDY those methods described on SUNDAYS, MEDITATE on

those godly aspects on MONDAY, and TRUST that God will provide for us on TUESDAYS. On WEDNESDAYS, let us WORK for the Lord faithfully as we struggle through life's challenges. On THURSDAYS, TRAVERSE or navigate to avoid those distractions that might keep us from holiness. As FRIDAY rolls around, FIGHT against those forces the evil one throws in our path daily, then SHOW our faith and commitment to God on SATURDAYS. While I mention all these actions on various days of the week, I do not mean to infer these are only necessary on those days; we ought to practice each of these daily. How much better prepared we could be to take up the shield of faith if we practice these attributes!

Mel Caraway

U.S. Army, Retired

Email: mgcaraway@comcast.net

CHAPTER SEVEN

BONE DOME

"And take the helmet of salvation." (Ephesians 6:17a. All Bible versions are noted.)

Throughout my military career as a U.S. Navy Hospital (i.e., Medical) Corpsman serving with the United States Marine Corps, many processes and actions became muscle memory—just a subconscious act because of continual practice. The way I prepared to go on patrol, either in training or in kinetic action, was no different. I would first don my utilities (e.g., working uniform), then my boots, then my flak jacket. The last item I would put on before picking up my weapon was my Kevlar helmet! Interestingly, this ordered process is referred to throughout the "Armor of God" passage we are now studying (this distinction will be examined more closely later in our survey). This chapter will discuss "taking the helmet of salvation" in the order mentioned. The helmet is the oldest form of protection for the warfighter. First recorded with the Akkadians (Semitic nomads, originating from the Arabian Peninsula, one of the most critical peoples in ancient Mesopotamia) around 2300 B.C., and was designed to protect the wearer's skull, which houses the brain. [1]

SPIRITUAL
BATTLE · RATTLE

Throughout my naval career as a "Devil Doc" serving with the Marine Corps, I referred to the skull as the "brain housing group" or "dome" (hence, *bone dome*). The brain is the center of all thought, emotion, and movement. Therefore, it is no surprise that Scripture would refer to the helmet of salvation as a protection for the believer's central organ of all life. In the sense of spiritual warfare, the helmet of salvation protects us from the snares and darts of Satan and against all false doctrines of man. But why is this item donned last? Why do we need a spiritual helmet in the first place? Are we not called unto His purpose? Are we not children of God? Are we, as those washed in the blood of Christ Jesus, not saved by faith through grace according to His word? Could it be that we always need to keep our helmet *on* and the chin strap *buckled* for another purpose? I propose Satan knows he has lost the battle but is still determined to win the war!

There is a slogan I repeatedly heard during my career: "Trample the weak and hurdle the dead!" Yes, it is very graphic, as are many of the slogans and mottos found within the arms profession. However, I can hear Satan saying the same thing! He is stalking his earthly prey as a lion stalks his target in the savannahs. In the opening verses of Job's book, God asks Satan where he has been (the Lord knew this as He is omniscient or all-knowing but wanted him to respond). Satan vaguely replies, "From going to and fro on the earth, and from walking back

and forth on it" (Job 1:7b, NKJV). The apostle Peter starkly states: "The devil walks about like a roaring lion, seeking whom he may devour" (1 Peter 5:8, NKJV).

Demons feast on the weary souls of those who have been downtrodden to the point of seemingly irreversible despair! We, as the called ones of God and washed in the blood of Christ, can find solace in our salvation. However, many Christians do not live as if they have been redeemed or have a hard time believing it for many reasons (or excuses): the daily grind of life, the emotional drain that we suffer from loss, from pain, from fatigue—even the complacency often found within the safety of being an heir to the Kingdom—all of which can give Satan and his demonic angels diverse opportunities they need to strike! Renner describes the protection, weight, and ornateness of the Roman military helmet. He says it was "etched with pastural scenes, with likenesses of animals, and with plumes of feathers and other material." [2] Often made of brass, it covered the entire skull to include the jaw and cheekbone. Given the material from which it was made, it was also cumbersome yet impenetrable by sword or battle-ax. Renner also likens Paul's analogous use of the helmet to explain salvation this way: "The ornateness of the ancient helmet was very difficult not to notice–often made of beautiful, shiny material; not unlike the salvation offered to us by our Savior!" [3]

SPIRITUAL BATTLE RATTLE

The ancient helmet was also a tight-fitting, protective item of armament for battle days. As mentioned previously, before going outside the wire (i.e., off base in Iraq), the last piece of weaponry I donned was my helmet. Once outside, I would rarely, if ever, remove my helmet. Occasionally I did, but at significant personal risk to myself and, indirectly, put my unit's safety in danger. In a spiritual sense, as the called ones of God, we often put our salvation at risk and, indirectly, the very souls of those whom we have called to discipleship by removing our helmets while outside the spiritual wire! Our helmet can, at times, feel heavy, hot, cumbersome, or even, at other times, seem meaningless.

We sometimes let our spiritual guard down, thinking we are in a safe place, perhaps a defilade (e.g., a military term for protective fortifications) of relative peace and protection. We often see the macro and micro terrains of this life and all its liberties and luxuries as our protection. Perhaps we find ourselves going about our day without a care in the world! All traffic lights are green on the way to work. We get that prime parking spot at the grocery store, or that much-needed bonus check shows up in the mail! Well, another saying used in military service is, "if an attack is going well, it's probably an ambush!" Remember, our adversary, the devil, wants us to let our spiritual guard down! He wants to lull us into a false sense of security while in

immortal spiritual combat, lay back on our pack, set our weapon down for a minute, and remove our helmet!

Think about those excuses we are sometimes tricked into using to remove our helmet of salvation—even for a moment: it is hot and heavy! Is it really? Or is that another tactic of Satan? Did Jesus not say in Matthew 11:29-30, 'Take My yoke upon you and learn of me; for I am meek and lowly in heart: and ye will find rest unto your souls. For my yoke is easy and my burden is light" (KJV)?

The snares of the devil are many! "Your salvation is too hard! Go out! Have some fun! Forget about all this spiritual stuff! You're good!" In case you are still confused about the "wiles of the Devil," consider what Genesis 3:4 says: "then the serpent said to the woman, 'You will not surely die'" (NKJV). Granted, it took Satan three times to tempt Eve to succumb to trickery, and it only took a suggestion from Eve for Adam to succumb to the same temptation. God has given us specific rules to live by, but Satan and his demon angels play a rather good PSY OPS game. He lulls us into letting our guard down, fills our minds with doubt, hurls darts of pain and worry and fear at us to the point we feel so exhausted that the easiest thing we can do is stop, take a knee, and remove the seemingly heavy and hot helmet and get some air!

This depiction of a soldier taking a moment to remove his helmet under fire reminds me of the scene in the movie *Saving Private Ryan*, when the U.S. Army was storming the beaches of Normandy, France, in World War Two. In this scene, a soldier was struck in the helmet by a ricochet round; he then stopped what he was doing and removed his helmet to inspect it. Taking his eyes off his enemy, even for that moment, proved fatal! While his helmet was off, another round struck him in the head, killing him instantly!

IT IS HOT!

Satan and his demonic army will use anything in their arsenal to cause us to submit, to succumb, to take a breath! In the hottest part of summer in Al Anbar, Iraq, in 2004, the ambient temperature hovered around 140 degrees Fahrenheit during the day and dropped to 90 to 100 degrees at night—that was HOT! Inside the wire was a little different. Our protective posture, or what Lieutenant Colonel Stephen "Godfather" Fernando in the HBO series "Generation Kill" referred to as "grooming standards," could be somewhat lax. However, outside the compound, we were in full combat kit or gear—flak vest, helmet, boots, and weapon. Water and individual communication (ICOM) radios were also necessary, as were items required to perform our job. As a Navy hospital corpsman or medic, my duty meant lugging all my medical gear plus ammunition for my service weapon. During the high

heat of the day, all this gear made our trudging through the countryside rough.

In the sense of spiritual warfare, it can get "hot" as well! Catching "heat" from our friends, coworkers, associates, and sometimes even family members can be challenging as we trudge along in life. But take heart! Our Lord is with us and will give us comfort. Isaiah 49:10 says, "They will not hunger or thirst. Nor will the scorching sun strike them down; for He who has compassion on them will lead them and will guide them to the springs of water."

Regardless of whether your particular battle is a true-life kinetic (i.e., dynamic) action or spiritual warfare, or both, take heart! The One who "has compassion" will shelter you and hydrate you! Satan is out to destroy your will and, eventually, your eternal soul! Always keep your helmet of salvation on! Our Lord God wants you to find and maintain peace and safety through Christ Jesus!

IT IS HEAVY!

As mentioned earlier, while outside the wire, we were in complete combat kit or gear—boots, "cammies" (e.g., camouflage uniforms), belt, flak jacket, helmet, weapon, ammo, water source, food, and, in my case, a medical bag full of lifesaving goodies! I never weighed my gear (I probably did not want to know); however, someone told me it

SPIRITUAL
BATTLE   RATTLE

hovered around 70 to 80 pounds. I went on about 60 combat patrols during that 2004 deployment. I weighed myself when I returned home and found I had not lost an ounce; I did, however, move that weight around a bit! I had gotten a lot stronger and my endurance vastly improved. Yes, the gear was heavy! But I adapted to it, and it changed me physically!

The trials we endure daily through perseverance and faith change us spiritually! Another aspect of patrolling is a relatively common practice called "spread loading," which shares your load or burden and allows your team to help carry it. I ordered my junior Navy corpsmen to "spread load" their medical gear throughout their fire team, squad, or platoon. It was also imperative they train their Marines in basic and sometimes advanced lifesaving skills. We shared ammunition, carried another Marine or sailor's gear, relieving each other, however temporarily, of each other's burden! The biblical analogy is remarkable! Galatians 6:2 teaches that we are to "bear one another's burdens, and so fulfill the law of Christ" (NKJV). Bearing one another's burdens or struggles can also have an added benefit. Sharing the load can also make the "armor of God" not seem secularly cumbersome! Having like-minded and directed individuals around you can make a tremendous difference in how we perceive our daily calling!

From a noncombatant or civilian sense, there is no difference! Temptation, death, sickness, trials, and tribulations can affect the most ardent and well-trained "soldier," causing great despair, fatigue (mentally and physically), and the strong desire to pack it in; to call in a real or symbolic extract. Sadly, many of my military friends have succumbed to suicide, and far more have been "lost" to drugs and alcohol, separating them from those who genuinely care and can help! While our earthly abilities to sustain and resist are fleeting, there is one who is called the Great Physician. While the experiences we, as a select few of society, can use to reach our fellow warriors' body and mind (even those who have not served in the military), there is One who can connect to the very soul! However, we must be ready at all times. We should never succumb to complacency in the Kingdom!

In summary, God's Word commands us to *take* the helmet of salvation–and wear it! Webster defines "take" to mean, in part, "to get into one's hands or into one's possession, power, or control." [4] The helmet of salvation is ours for the taking! We must "take" possession of it or grasp it. Seize possession of this gift of God through His Son, place it on your spiritual head, and never remove it!

Eric Owens

U.S. Naval Reserve, Retired (Devil Doc)

Email: doc.owens@comcast.net

CHAPTER EIGHT

WEAPON TRAINING

"And take ... the sword of the Spirit, which is the word of God."
(Ephesians 6:17. All Scriptures are from the English Standard Version,
except where noted.)

There are forces at work in the world that are adamantly opposed
to God and His purposes. Such parties produce great conflict between
God's representatives and evil forces. As set forth by Jesus Christ,
God's mission for believers brings this conflict into the life of every
committed disciple of Christ. However, disciples are assured of victory
because Christ remains King, and God will achieve His predetermined
purposes. This assurance is possible because His disciples are armed
with God's spiritual powers, as outlined in Ephesians chapter six.

Christians can succeed in this spiritual warfare against evil forces
when they depend upon God's spiritual powers and not
themselves. The charge is, "Be strong in the Lord and in the strength
of his might" (Ephesians 6:10). Strength to resist evil is found only in
the vital energy that comes from being united with the Lord. Such

power from Him assures us we can, in Paul's words, be "more than conquerors" (Romans 8:37; cf. Philippians 4:13).

Believers of past generations in America have witnessed the power of evil. It was revealed in the 1930s as Adolf Hitler's thirst for power and kingdoms motivated him to march across Europe to conquer the world. The Nazi army marched across multiple countries with its tanks and armaments' weapons. Many of these nations fought back, yet they lacked the workforce and weaponry necessary to defeat this evil. These nations fell because they lacked the weapons and sufficient power to equip them for such a battle.

World War Two in Europe is parallel in many ways to the battle that believers face in their spiritual warfare with the world today. Yet, many are not even aware of the spiritual warfare going on. Furthermore, those who discover the war in which they are involved are not aware of God's spiritual weapons that He is ready to issue to ensure victory in the battle against evil freely.

Through the Apostle Paul, the Holy Spirit summons Christians to clothe themselves in the very spiritual armor of God—a call to duty (Ephesians 6:11). To meet the spiritual forces of evil, the disciple of Christ must take upon himself all that God provides. He enabled King David to overcome the mightier weapons and strength of the giant

Goliath because of his simple faith in the power of God. This young king cried out to Goliath: "You come to me with a sword and with a spear and with a javelin, but I come to you in the name of the LORD of hosts" (1 Samuel 17:45).

The need for God's armor is evident when one realizes that this battle is "against the wiles of the devil." These powers of the devil are much stronger than we might imagine. The devil is deceptive, appearing as a "roaring lion" (1 Peter 5:8) at times and as an "angel of light" (2 Corinthians 11:14) at other times. According to the Scriptures, the devil beguiles, seduces, opposes, resists, deceives, hinders, tempts, persecutes, and blasphemes. He is the "prince of the power of the air" (Ephesians 2:2) and the "god of this world" (2 Corinthians 4:4).

When we read of the "wiles of the devil," we tend to think that this is so much superstition. In the second century, there were many tortures inflicted upon Christians, which they thought were the devil's works. Polycarp wrote, "The devil tried many devices against them (Christians–*tls*). But thanks be to God, his might did not prevail over any." [1] The churches at Lyons and Vienne, France tell of persecutions against their members. Those people spoke of "the greatness of the tribulation in this region and the fury of the heathen against the saints." From that era, writers ascribed all evil as being from the devil:

For with all his might the adversary fell upon us, giving a foretaste of his unbridled activity at his future coming … But the grace of God led the conflict against him, and delivered the weak, and set them as firm pillars, able through patience to endure all the wrath of the Evil One. [2]

Our secular society may not believe in the devil anymore, but he remains just as powerful in our world as he was in the ancient world. The greatest gift in the world for the devil would be for us not to believe in him, for this would give him a freer rein to move in this present age. But be sure that the Evil one remains alive and well, irrespective of whether we believe in him or not.

The truth is the devil appears in more sophisticated ways today for a more sophisticated audience. Today, Satan is known for the guise of false pleasure, materialism, corrupt politics, etc. He is indeed alive and well today and continues to use his limited power to deceive, yes, even the elect (i.e., Christians). Therefore, Paul's word is ever relevant: "For we are not contending against flesh and blood, but against the principalities, against the powers, against the world rulers of this present darkness, against the spiritual hosts of wickedness in the heavenly places" (Ephesians 6:12, RSV). Would it not be the height of folly to try in our strength to resist such an opponent? The deadly forces of evil would easily overwhelm us if we tried to repel them without the armor of God.

Throughout your study of this book, you have been introduced to some of the armaments of God's armor. This chapter points out one such weapon, "the sword of the Spirit." Realizing the formidable and threatening presence of the powerful devil in our lives, the Evil One seeking to destroy our eternal life, how can we use the sword of the Spirit in our battle?

Paul's charge here: "Having done all … take the sword of the Spirit, which is the word of God" (Ephesians 6:13, 17). Notice this weapon is not ours, but the Holy Spirit's. We cannot forge the sword, design it, or sharpen it—we can only use it. Additionally, the sword of the Spirit is the word of God. The Greek word here for "sword" is *machaira*, a short sword or *defensive* weapon to be used openly in the face of any attack.

Notice above that the sword is a *defensive* weapon. Paul's charge in Ephesians six is, "Therefore take the whole armor of God, that you may be able to *withstand*, and having done all, to *stand*. *Stand* therefore" (v. 13-14a, emphasis mine, *tls*). The short sword (*machaira*) was used in the Roman army as a defense weapon, not for offense but for protection. Thus, Paul's order is to "stand our ground" in our battle against the devil. It is God's power to bring us to victory. Only the Holy Spirit of God can make this weapon (e.g., the Scriptures) effective. This particular weapon is the good news of the death, burial,

resurrection, and ascension to the right hand of God, our Lord and Savior Jesus Christ. Amid the battle, these facts assure the believer that he or she will be delivered and their enemy vanquished.

It is of utmost importance here to note that in warfare, believers do not overcome the "world rulers of this present darkness," but that God alone can win the victory. Christians do no more than remain standing in a battle that God alone can win. The armor of God allows one to stand firm. No shouts of victory are to emerge from the believer's mouths, for the success belongs to God, not to us. Prayers of thanksgiving for God's grace are the only appropriate response:

> Praying at all times in the Spirit, with all prayer and supplication. To that end, keep alert with all perseverance, making supplication for all the saints, and also for me, that words may be given to me in opening my mouth boldly to proclaim the mystery of the gospel, for which I am an ambassador in chains, that I may declare it boldly, as I ought to speak." (Ephesians 6:18-20, ESV)

This brings us to the critical question concerning the "sword of the Spirit," that being, "How do we effectively use this 'sword,' or 'Word of God'"? When I joined the Marine Corps as a young lad of seventeen, fresh out of high school, I was not a Christian. Yet, sometime after my enlistment, I was issued a pocket-size New Testament. I do not have it today, but I do remember it was Marine-

green, with a Marine Corps emblem on the front cover. I do not recall ever reading that Testament. However, every time I was in a situation that made me feel uneasy, facing some danger, etc., I always took this small book with me, either in my gear or my pocket. This book became my talisman, supposedly keeping me free from evil and safe from harm. I carried this New Testament Bible with me in such situations, superstitiously thinking it would protect me from all evil.

I fear that many today look at the Scriptures in much the same way. We have the Bible on our coffee tables, in our libraries, on our phones, carry it to church, etc., but rarely open the Book of books to discover its meaning and message for us and our lives. It is a comfort in our day-to-day activities, and, in our present time, the Bible remains the best-selling book in the entire world, creating sales of between $425-650 million annually. So again, we ask, "How do we take this sword of the Spirit and use it effectively as God's offensive weapon in our spiritual battle against the devil?" We dare not fail to do so, dare not ignore the importance of God's power available to us in Christ.

The significant change in my life came when I worked for the U.S. government in Europe, following service in the Marine Corps. It was here that I meet a Christian missionary in Lausanne, Switzerland. This individual's lifestyle and commitment to Christ was so impressive to me. In turn, he opened the Scriptures up to me, challenging me to

become engaged in reading, studying, and applying them to my life. As is the typical story for many Christians, when one exposes himself to the Word of God, His power begins its work on our hearts (cf. Romans 1:16-17); and so, I was baptized into Christ in 1966.

As we have seen thus far in this study, Paul's letter to the Ephesians is perhaps the most explicit definition of the spiritual war that believers are engaged in with the devil. In this letter, the apostle warns us that apart from the weapons God has provided for us, we are without hope in this battle. My recommendation to all who desire to use the gift of God's "sword of the Spirit" is to initially make Ephesians chapters four through six a significant part of your life. In this book, you will find how to open your life to God's power. During this journey, you will encounter what spiritual gifts you have received, how to avoid the world's deceptiveness, and how to use your talents to produce spiritual strength.

In Ephesians, Paul addresses how to use God's power and gift to produce a better home, family, and social life. You will learn how to live in holiness, purity, honesty, and obedience. Christians will also discover that God is their sole source for obedience, truth, and sacrificial living. We will then grow, as did Christ, "in wisdom and in stature, and in favor with God and man" (Luke 2:52).

In the Marine Corps, every individual is foremost a *warrior*. Therefore, we were taught the importance of our weapons. Every Marine, enlisted and officer, is trained in proper rifle usage and maintenance. Additionally, all Marines memorize the "Rifleman's Creed," created in 1942 by Brigadier General William H. Rupertus. He wrote to Marines, "that the only weapon which stands between them and death is the rifle … they must understand that their rifle is their life." [3]

Similarly, every Christian must recognize that he or she always stands in harm's way concerning the Evil One. Therefore, we must be trained entirely in the knowledge and use of God's "sword of the Spirit." When we lay down our swords and neglect the study and application of the words of God, we wind up losing our spiritual battle against the devil.

Many of us are weak and ineffective at standing our ground against the attacks of the devil because we, unlike the Roman soldier, have no skill in handling our swords. In contrast, every time we pick up the word of God, study and apply it to our daily life, the greater our God-given victory (-ies) will be. This is why it is so important to correctly handle and rightly divide the sword of the Spirit (cf. 2 Timothy 2:15). This sword is God's way of assuring the Christians victory over spiritual death.

We close with Paul's command: "Finally, be strong in the Lord and in the strength of his might. Put on the whole armor of God, that you may be able to stand against the schemes of the devil … And take … the sword of the Spirit, which is the word of God" (Ephesians 6:10-11, 17).

Tom Seals

U.S. Marine Corps, Veteran

Email: tom@godsword-forwarriors.org

(EDITOR'S NOTE: Tom is the Founder / Chairman of the Board, *God's Word For Warriors*, a non-profit organization serving military veterans struggling with elements of moral and spiritual injury due to military-related trauma and hardships. For more information, go to godswordforwarriors.com.)

CHAPTER NINE

SECURE NETWORK

"And pray in the Spirit on all occasions with all kinds of   prayers and requests.   With this in mind,   be   alert and always   keep on praying for all the Lord's people." (Ephesians 6:18. All Scriptures are from the New International Version unless otherwise noted.)

Often when a soldier is deployed to a combat location, they feel the most worth when they contribute to the fight. There are many jobs in the U.S. Army that do the same thing, whether in theater or not. But even those jobs seem more relevant when in the combat zone. Whether on a battleground or in garrison, you always need a secure communication network. However, I will focus on the combat zone for our purposes in this book because I feel we are in a real spiritual battle. We all have an essential role in this conflict, no matter our particular speciality.

The U.S. military uses the latest technology for secure satellite communications. "Communication technology is evolving rapidly, changing the way military forces communicate but also creating new threats." [1]

The U.S. Army's Warfighter Information Network Tactical programme (WIN-T) is the army's current 'tactical network backbone', according to manufacturer General Dynamics. It offers soldiers secure voice and data communications on the battlefield without the need for fixed infrastructure. First deployed in Iraq in 2004, WIN-T meant soldiers 'had a high-speed, interoperable voice and data communications network at the battalion level'... It offered soldiers the ability to stream real-time video, view a topographical map of friendly forces, send texts requesting medical assistance, digitally call for artillery support, and access mission command apps like Command Post of the Future and Tactical Ground Reporting System. [2]

While I was deployed to Afghanistan and Iraq, we had two communication networks: a low and a high side which correlates to an *unclassified* and a *secret* (classified) side. While both systems are highly protected, the secret network is even more secure and harder to hack and gain unauthorized access. However, our adversaries continually try to penetrate, exploit, and destroy our communication systems.

Ephesians 6:18 says we are to "pray in the Spirit all occasions with all kinds of prayers and requests." We must know and believe that it is on a secure network when we pray. I think you can pray "in the spirit" when you are in Christ and believe that He hears you. 1 Peter 3:12 says, "For the eyes of the Lord are toward the righteous, and His ears attend to their prayer, but the face of the Lord is against evildoers"

(NASB). Those who are righteous are in Christ, so it is not a righteousness we earned, but one given us because of our faith in Christ. I believe that He hears everyone's prayers, but He is even more attentive when His faithful followers pray to Him.

The Army's secure or secret side is where we converse about times, dates, and locations we do not want our enemy to know. It is a safe place to talk more freely and openly about our plans and purposes. The same thing goes for our prayer life. It is not secure because one can hear or break into this network it is protected in the sense that we can have complete confidence that God is listening! Our safeguarded network is our time alone with God. It is the means whereby we can be open and honest with Him and communicate the innermost part of ourselves. Now that is *absolute* security!

Verse 18 of the Ephesian letter also says to "pray in the Spirit on all occasions with all kinds of prayers and requests." The New International Version translates the Greek word *deeseos* as "requests," which I think tones down this passage's meaning. This word means "praying for a *specific, felt need…* [a] heart-*felt* petition, arising out of deep personal need (sense of lack, want)." [3] This text tells us to be specific and detailed in presenting our needs via prayer. Even if we may sound selfish, God wants our needs or requests to come from the heart because Romans 8:26 tells us "the Spirit helps us in our weakness. We

do not know what we ought to pray for, but the Spirit himself intercedes for us through wordless groans." So, if we are pouring our heart to Him in prayer, He will hear us, and His Spirit will help present our prayers to God to make them suitable and holy. Whether you pray to Him when you are happy, sad, or even angry, God wants to hear from you more than anything, as the passage says, "in all occasions."

The second half of Ephesians 6:18 tells us, "with this in mind, be alert and always keep on praying for all the Lord's people." Knowing that God hears us and wants us to pray to Him on all occasions with various kinds of prayers, do not forget to pray for your fellow Christian brothers and sisters! Even though we can be selfish and angry sometimes when we pray to God, the writer says do not be so selfish that you forget others because they need your prayers.

Prayer is so *simple* and yet so *complicated*. Simple in that, we need to talk to God and tell Him what is on our minds and ask Him for things we need. But, complicated in that if we ask Him for what we need, why do other Christians need to ask God on our behalf for the same thing? God already knows, right? In some supernatural way that we may never understand in this life, God's power is magnified when we pray to Him in our quiet place and when others are praying for us in their quietness or alone time with God. We know from passages like Acts 4:31 that there is substantial power when Christians pray together! That Bible

verse says, "when they had prayed, the place where they had gathered together was shaken, and they were all filled with the Holy Spirit and began to speak the word of God with boldness" (NASB). Prayer is complex in that we do not know precisely why it is more powerful when we all pray about the same thing, whether together or in our quiet place. Does God somehow get influenced because we are all asking for the same thing? That could be part of it.

When my children were younger and they all asked to eat at a particular restaurant, I was more inclined to go there. Is it because God sees unity among the saints when praying for the same thing? I do not mean in a corporate or church worship setting either. I believe that is most powerful. Even though our family is separated from one another, God is omnipresent (i.e., all present everywhere) and can hear them simultaneously. So that unity among us is pleasing to God. It is hard to grasp how it works fully but, we should always believe and feel "secure" because it does work and that He hears every single word and petition.

In the Army (and all military branches), we plan our courses of action to send up the command chain. And just because it is on a secure network does not mean that it will make it up to the Commander-in-Chief (e.g., President of the United States). If we knew we had direct access to the CINC, we might be a little selfish and would

probably request things and communicate with him daily. However, in our spiritual network, we have access to our spiritual Commander and Chief: our Heavenly Father. 24/7/365! God listens to every "little" prayer we may have. He is listening to every kind word or angry word. And the Spirit will show Him our heart, which is the most important thing of all. Why was King David a man after God's own heart? We all know his flaws and sins that he committed. Despite his faults, he never gave up his belief that God loved him and that He was faithful even though David was not.

We may believe that just because we have committed what we consider a horrible sin, God cannot or will not forgive us, or He will hold it against us. And this will probably affect our prayer life. To God, however, no sin is unredeemable if we repent. We may still feel bad for what we have done but, when we ask in faith for God's forgiveness, He is faithful and grants us His mercy. The apostle John says, "If we confess our sins, he is faithful and just and will forgive us our sins and purify us from all unrighteousness" (1 John 1:9, NIV). So, brothers and sisters, never believe the lies that Satan and the world will hurl at you, such as God could never forgive you. Sadly, this is one of the most effective ways that Satan deceives us and keeps us from communicating with our heavenly Commander-in-Chief; he tries to make us think that God would not dare listen to a sinner like me. Do

not give up on one of your best weapons against Satan and his evil forces: *prayer*. This mode of transmission, coupled with quiet time with God and meditating on His Word, is one of the most effective ways to keep us in tune with Him, to give us the strength we need to carry on and is a powerful way to send help to those brothers and sisters in harm's way in this spiritual life and death battle.

We are presently in a great spiritual battle in our country, possibly the most critical conflict of our lifetime. The forces of good and evil are clashing all around. We must remember that we have a *secure* line directly to the Master of the Universe! He will never leave us or forsake us (Deuteronomy 31:6; Matthew 28:20b; Hebrews 13:5). Though we can see many casualties of the spiritual battle, we must never lose heart! When Joshua was appointed leader of the Israelite nation following Moses' death, God reassured him: "Have I not commanded you? Be strong and courageous. Do not be afraid; do not be discouraged, for the LORD your God will be with you wherever you go" (Joshua 1:9). Before crossing into the Promised Land of Canaan, their Commander-in-Chief (and ours) pronounced His promise to be present with Joshua and Israel no less than three times in this context.

Additionally, God encouraged His people via Joshua to be "strong and courageous" four times in this same chapter. In this present day and time in which we live, we desperately need to read and relish in

God's divine message of strength and courage in the face of constant assault from Satan and his evil forces. Daily interaction with our heavenly Father via prayer and diligent study of the scriptures will keep our hope firmly anchored in Him rather than the decaying world around us.

We must also pray for our fellow soldiers in Christ and never leave a fallen comrade, no matter where he or she might be. God loves us despite our faults! He forgives us even though we may not feel like we do not deserve it! Even in our darkest times, believe that God is faithful and know that we have a Secure Network where we can always directly contact our heavenly Commander and Chief who cares for us!

In armed combat, there are many battle casualties or combat injuries. Many of those physical scars will heal with time. However, many wounds are emotional and spiritual in nature, which do not fade as quickly. Many soldiers carry the burden of wondering, "Why did I make it back alive and not my comrade or battle buddy?" Those are difficult things to have seen and experienced, but soldiers must get help to carry on and not live with the guilt of "why." While engaged in spiritual battle, may we never carry the guilt of wondering what more we could have done to save a brother or sister in Christ from the Evil One. We have one of the most potent tools or weapons. The power of prayer is the easiest to do but, many times, the least used. Why is

this? Why do many not believe in the power of prayer? I think it is because we may assume that if our prayers are unanswered simply because God has not granted us our request. We do not understand that the power is not in our request but rather our faith in God from whom we are requesting. Faith and prayer go hand in hand.

When we cease to pray, we have begun our path to unbelief. When we do not initiate contact with God, we begin to lose hold of our faith. Praying on all occasions, with all kinds of prayers and requests as our passage implores us, may sometimes mean that we pray even when we do not feel like it. It means being intentional and disciplined so that we never lose contact with one of the primary weapons in our arsenal against the forces of evil.

In closing, as previously mentioned, we are presently in a spiritual battle that may be the most important one of our lifetimes, as the forces of good and evil are clashing all around us (and even within us). While we will see many battle casualties, we must never lose heart! Even in our darkest times, we must believe that God is faithful and know that we have a Secure Network where we always have direct contact with our heavenly Commander-in-Chief who cares for us. Unlike our military's communication network that faces constant threats, we can always trust that our communication with God—

prayer—is secure and never vulnerable to Satan's evil intentions. May the peace of Christ be with you always!!!

Albert Flores

U.S. Army, Active Duty (Religious Affairs NCO)

Email: alpat12@yahoo.com

CHAPTER TEN

GUARD DUTY

"And pray in the Spirit on all occasions with all kinds of prayers and requests. With this in mind, *be alert* and always keep on praying for all the Lord's people." (Ephesians 6:18, All Scriptures noted are from the New International Version unless otherwise noted.)

"Heaven and earth will pass away, but my words will never pass away. But about that day or hour no one knows, not even the angels in heaven, nor the Son, but only the Father. Be on guard! *Be alert!* You do not know when that time will come." (Mark 13:31)

"*Be alert* and of sober mind. Your enemy the devil prowls around like a roaring lion looking for someone to devour." (1 Peter 5:8. Emphases in all three verses are mine, *ds*)

Many Christians are waiting for Jesus Christ to return—but not many are alert and watching for His reappearance! The Bible does not teach us to merely wait for Him; we are to be on the lookout! What is the difference between waiting and watching? Which would you rather have when the enemy might attack—someone on guard duty who is merely waiting for the enemy to show up or someone on guard duty who is watching to see if the enemy has shown up? The difference

between "waiting" and "watching" here might mean the difference between life and death! (*source unknown*)

The Bible teaches we are to be wide awake watching for the return of Jesus, not just waiting for Him. Those who watch will keep themselves alert and self-controlled; those who only wait may let their guard down! As soldiers of the cross, we must realize that while we are waiting for the Lord to return, we should remain alert and on guard because our enemy, Satan, is still trying to take prisoners. We must stay alert and keep a good lookout for Satan's attacks while watching for the Lord's appearance.

In Gideon's victory over the Midianites, the surprise element played a prominent part. Gideon surprised and defeated an enemy of 135,000 warriors with a mere three hundred men. Pearl Harbor's attack is another good lesson in the benefit of surprise and what happens when we are not alert and on guard. To face the attacks that Satan brings against us, we must always be on guard and remove his element of surprise. In his *Principles of War*, Wilson points out that the enemy's intelligence ensures knowing who he is, his intentions, and his operation methods. [1]

Twenty times in the New Testament, God instructs Christians to be watchful. In most cases, it is Jesus who commands it. Failure to

follow these instructions resulted in the eleven disciples experiencing defeat in Gethsemane. On another occasion, Jesus said to them, "What I say unto you, I say unto all. Watch!" (Mark 13:37). Although Christ spoke these words relative to His return, the warning also applies to our battles with our spiritual adversary. Against what forces are we to be watchful, alert, and on guard? We are engaged in a spiritual war, and we have a very formidable adversary! God said, in Genesis 3:15 that "I will put enmity between you and the woman, and between your seed and her seed; he shall crush your head, and you will bruise His heel." This enmity, conflict, or war – between Satan and the seed or descendants of Eve – has been ongoing since the fall of man in the Garden of Eden.

In previous chapters, we have examined the armor God has provided to be prepared to stand against our enemy. Some armor pieces are for the offense as we attack our adversary, while some are defensive for our protection. What comes after fully donning God's armor? Do we just sit back and wait for the inevitable attack of Satan to come? I suggest we cannot afford to wait. We must be on guard, alert, and watchful! If we fall asleep, even though clothed in our spiritual battle rattle that God has provided, our adversary may strike a death blow. We need to review the spiritual warfare in which we are engaged. The better prepared we are, the more likely we are to

withstand Satan's attacks and survive the enmity between him and us and rejoice in the Lord's return.

What is "spiritual warfare?" While this term is nowhere in Scripture, the concept is. Paul wrote two of the most associated passages:

> For though we live in the world, we do not wage war as the world does. The weapons we fight with are not the weapons of the world. On the contrary, they have divine power to demolish strongholds. We demolish arguments and every pretension that sets itself up against the knowledge of God and we take captive every thought to make it obedient to Christ. (2 Corinthians 10:3-5)

And,

> Finally, be strong in the Lord and in His mighty power. Put on the full armor of God so that you can take your stand against the devil's schemes. For our struggle is not against flesh and blood, but against the rulers, against the authorities, against the powers of this dark world and against the spiritual forces of evil in the heavenly realms." (Ephesians 6:10-12)

Too many Christians have become passive and fearful. Some are satisfied just to believe the right things and attend church services and activities each week. This lifestyle differs significantly from that which Jesus called believers to live. In this warfare, we actively resist the devil. We actively pursue spiritual disciplines that will strengthen us and be

better prepared. We actively engage the enemy when people are in spiritual bondage. We use prayer as a weapon to penetrate strongholds that cannot be reached any other way. Spiritual warfare is putting aside passive attitudes towards faith, which keeps us from commitment and causes us to pursue only those things that will benefit us. Instead of seeking our agenda, we submit our will to God in spiritual warfare and accept the sacrifices He calls us to make. Brothers and sisters, we are at war!

The Bible serves as the battle manual for God's army. It outlines by instruction and illustration the specific schemes used by Satan to trap us. Our opponent is highly skilled, with over 5,000 years of experience. We cannot destroy our opponent, but we can keep him from being successful in his attacks against us. No victorious military strategist would enter battle without first having a thorough understanding of the adversary. Since God has provided us with vivid accounts of Satan's past exploits, we are without excuse if surprise catches us. [2] You and I are engaged in an actual battle. We know we are facing a real opponent because this world bears the bloody, painful scars of the conflict: war among nations, shattered lives, broken homes, suicide, rape, abuse, and immorality of every kind.

No war in history can compare with the battle we are fighting. I am talking about the spiritual warfare that we became a part of when we

put our Lord on in baptism. There is no way we can avoid this conflict. There is no place where we can hide that can shield us from the effects of this battle between God and his forces and Satan and his forces. Since we are at war, there is so much at stake both now and in eternity; we must find out what spiritual warfare is about and how to fight successfully. Satan is not alone fighting the dark side of this battle: he has a host of followers, angels, and demons. Scripture tells us that when he rebelled against God, Satan took one-third of the angels with him. We are up against a formidable foe that we need to understand and take seriously.

Do you believe God, Jesus, and Satan are real? "Real" means genuine compared to false or factual compared to make-believe. The Bible reveals that God, Jesus, and Satan are real, not myths. Satan is a veritable force with whom we must contend. He is not a being with horns, a tail, and a pitchfork wearing a red suit—that would be too obvious. He is subtle, crafty, and sneaky. Satan's greatest trick is to convince the world that he does not exist. In 1 Peter 5:8, we are warned to "Be alert and of sober mind. Your enemy the devil prowls around like a roaring lion looking for someone to devour." We are his targets, and he is out to get us (review Chapter Three, "Military Intelligence," for additional details).

Spiritual warfare is a battle of the mind and heart. God gives light and truth; Satan tries his best to cloud light and truth with darkness and lies. His primary tool is deception, convincing humans that the lies they believe are the truth. God will allow you to believe Satan's lies. That was the first step in Eve's sin. The very essence of spiritual warfare is lies versus truth. Satan and his angels go all out to get us to love their lies more than we love the truth of God. Since Satan and his angels cannot *make* you do anything, they try to find a way to delude and lead you to disobey God. They wage war to confuse your mind and capture our heart.

While Satan is formidable, he is not all-powerful; he is not everywhere; he is not all-knowing. He is not an equal to God, only evil. He is far less than God. He is a created being, and therefore has limited capacities. His abilities are far greater than people's abilities but far less than God's capabilities. Satan's power does not lie in his ability to *make* us do anything but in his ability to tempt us and our weaknesses to give in to these temptations (James 1:13-15). Satan only has power where we are weak. If we are strong and resist, he will flee from us (James 4:7). However, Satan can know our weaknesses and tempt us with just the right things that will lead us to sin against God. Satan is big, bad, and mad, but he is not God. He is NOT God. He is a rogue angel gone bad and is not on par with God.

Note three attributes about God: <u>first</u>, He is *omnipotent*, all-powerful. Satan is not—his power is limited. He could not attack Job or Peter without permission. When kicked out of heaven, he could not force his way back in. When Satan attacked Jesus at His birth, the angel Michael (Revelation chapter 12) defeated Satan; thus, his power is restricted. "No temptation has seized you except what is common to man. And God is faithful; he will not let you be tempted beyond what you can bear. But when you are tempted, he will also provide a way out so that you can stand up under it" (1 Corinthians 12:13). <u>Second</u>, God is *omnipresent* — He is everywhere, Satan is not. Like any other angel, Satan can be in only one place at a time. He has other angels to help. And <u>third</u>, God is *omniscient* in that He knows all. Satan does not. Matthew 24:36 tells us that angels do not know everything. Even though God limits Satan, he is still a powerful foe for humans. "For our struggle is not against flesh and blood, but against the rulers, against the authorities, against the powers of this dark world and against the spiritual forces of evil in the heavenly realms" (Ephesians 6:12).

We are involved whether we realize it or not and have no choice. Satan wants each of us. He has no scruples and will do anything. We are at war. Unseen beings influence us, either for good or for evil. Because their influence is so powerful, we must search the Scriptures

to understand these evil forces and what they do. Without an awareness of which urgings come from good forces versus those from evil powers, we may find ourselves in situations without the wisdom we need to make the right decisions. [3] In his book *Satan, His Motive and Methods*, Chafer offers some excellent observations regarding Satan's system:

> Though under the restraining hand of God, Satan, according to scriptures, is in authority over the unregenerate world, and the unsaved are unconsciously organized and federated under his leading … In at least thirty passages, the English word 'world' is again used … the world of men, their evil undertakings, ideals, and federation. This federation includes all the unsaved and fallen humanity; it has the cooperation of the fallen spirits, and is but the union of all who are living and acting in independence of God. This satanic system has its own ideals and principles which are in sharp contrast to the ideals and principles given the redeemed. [4]

Chafer also details some facts concerning this satanic system: (1) *Satan is the governing head* (cf. 1 John 4:4; 1 John 5:19). We have no power to fight Satan except the outside. Man has attempted to fight Satan through various methods such as education, legislation, environment, and organizations. Satan has even turned some of these to his favor (e.g., law & abortion). (2) *The Satanic system is wholly evil.* Many will deny this statement, but we can see it is right compared to God's holiness.

SPIRITUAL BATTLE BATTLE

(3) *The same world that crucified Christ will also hate the saved one in whom He dwells.* (4) *Jesus is the only one strong enough to break the power of Satan.* It is only through His gospel that people can be set free. He is the solution to our problem of sin (cf. Acts 26:16-18). [5] The religious author, C. S. Lewis, once said, "no clever arrangement of bad eggs can make a good omelet." [6] Consider the following Scriptures:

Luke 11:21-22, "When a strong man, fully armed, guards his own house, his possessions are safe. But when someone stronger attacks and overpowers him, he takes away the armor in which the man trusted and divides up the spoils."

1 John 3:8, "He who does what is sinful is of the devil, because the devil has been sinning from the beginning. The reason the Son of God appeared was to destroy the devil's work."

Acts 26:16-18,

> Now get up and stand on your feet. I have appeared to you to appoint you as a servant and as a witness of what you have seen and will see of me. I will rescue you from your own people and from the Gentiles. I am sending you to them to open their eyes and turn them from darkness to light, and from the power of Satan to God, so that they may receive forgiveness of sins and a place among those who are sanctified by faith in me.

We either stand with Jesus or with Satan. If we say we do not support Satan, but we are not ready to accept Jesus totally, we are mistaken and endangering our lives. By not accepting Jesus, we accept Satan by default. We can choose to follow Jesus, or Satan will take us into his camp whether we decide, and we may not even know we are there. Jesus is the great divider in history and forces us to choose. There is not one Christian ministry area that has not become a battleground. It has become common to attribute a natural or human explanation to most problems and leave it at that.

The person who has a spiritual warfare perspective will be inclined to test the situation to determine whether there is something more than natural influences involved. A spiritual warrior is aware of the enemy's activities. Spiritual fighters also know they must discipline their thoughts and actions, taking sin seriously because he always deny the adversary an advantage. God's soldier must always be on guard against comparing himself with others and being entrapped by the subtlety of religious pride. The loyal warrior knows he can do nothing useful by his strength alone. His power, authority, wisdom, and discernment depend on his close walk with his Lord. He should always remain focused and guard himself against distractions caused by problems and troubles that appear. In other words, a commitment to spiritual warfare means we each need four new things:

1. A New Attitude: You begin to think like an overcomer with a victorious attitude. You realize you want to be on the front lines for God, not trying to live a comfortable life.

2. A Greater Focus: You recognize Satan likes to entangle God's people in the cares of this world or provoke us to react in fleshly ways.

3. A Necessary Discipline: You have begun to discipline yourself in all areas. You set aside more time for study and prayer.

4. A More Balanced Biblical World View: You take the Biblical warnings seriously to God's people about an enemy that is real.

While all this is true, we must still be watchful. We are to be sentries to protect ourselves and others. In the Bible, watchmen were security guards responsible for protecting towns and military installations from surprise enemy attacks and other potential dangers. Ancient Israelite cities often stationed security guards on high walls or in watchtowers. Their job was to keep watch and warn the townspeople of impending threats. The Hebrew word translated *watchman* means "one who looks out," "one who spies," or "one who watches." [7] Sometimes, these guards were scouts who looked out for approaching friends and enemies. There are many references to those who kept an eye out for physical threats in the Bible. "Now the watchman was standing on the tower in Jezreel, and he saw the company of Jehu as he came and said,

'I see a company.' And Joram said, 'Take a horseman and send to meet them, and let him say,' 'Is it peace?'" (2 Kings 9:17, English Standard Version). Watchmen safeguarded fields and vineyards during harvest time (Isaiah 5:1–2; Matthew 21:33; Mark 12:1) and acted as sentinels who announced the start of a new day (Psalm 130:6; Isaiah 21:11–12).

The Bible also refers to guards in a spiritual sense. God appointed prophets as spiritual guardians over the souls of His people: "Son of man, I have made you a watchman for the people of Israel; so hear the word I speak and give them warning from Me" (Ezekiel 33:7; also Hosea 9:8). The prophets' job as security guards was to urge God's people to live faithfully and warn them of the perils involved in falling away from the Lord and doing evil. As watchmen, the prophets were also called upon to warn wicked people of the judgment and destruction that would come their way unless they turned from their evil ways.

Israel's spiritual guardsmen bore a heavy responsibility before the Lord. If a prophet failed to warn others as God had appointed him to do, his own life was in danger, and he would be held accountable for the people's sin:

Son of man, speak to your people and say to them: 'When I bring the sword against a land, and the people of the land choose one of their men and make him their watchman, and he sees the

sword coming against the land and blows the trumpet to warn the people, then if anyone hears the trumpet but does not heed the warning and the sword comes and takes their life, their blood will be on their own head. Since they heard the sound of the trumpet but did not heed the warning, their blood will be on their own head. If they had heeded the warning, they would have saved themselves. If the watchman sees the sword coming and does not blow the trumpet to warn the people and the sword comes and takes someone's life, that person's life will be taken because of their sin, but I will hold the watchman accountable for their blood.' (Ezekiel 33:2–6)

A watchman who was blind or disobedient to the Lord's word left the people he was to protect open to danger and suffering (Isaiah 56:10). Obedience is the only course of action for a faithful guard: "But if you do warn the wicked person to turn from their ways and they do not do so, they will die for their sin, though you yourself will be saved" (Ezekiel 33:9). The role of spiritual watchmen continues in the New Testament as church leaders: "Obey your spiritual leaders and do what they say. Their work is to watch over your souls, and they are accountable to God. Give them reason to do this with joy and not with sorrow. That would certainly not be for your benefit" (Hebrews 13:17, NLT).

In another sense, God calls leaders and all Christians to be sentinels or guardians. Jesus told His disciples to "watch and pray so that you

will not fall into temptation. The spirit is willing, but the flesh is weak" (Mark 14:38). We should all be ready and waiting for the Lord's return:

> Be dressed ready for service and keep your lamps burning, like servants waiting for their master to return from a wedding banquet, so that when he comes and knocks they can immediately open the door for him. It will be good for those servants whose master finds them watching when he comes. Truly I tell you, he will dress himself to serve, will have them recline at the table and will come and wait on them. It will be good for those servants whose master finds them ready, even if he comes in the middle of the night or toward daybreak. But understand this: If the owner of the house had known at what hour the thief was coming, he would not have let his house be broken into. You also must be ready, because the Son of Man will come at an hour when you do not expect him. (Luke 12:35–40)

Moses recorded, "It was a night of watching by the LORD, to bring them out of the land of Egypt; so, this same night is a night of watching kept to the LORD by all the people of Israel throughout their generations" (Exodus 12:42, English Standard Version). God commanded that the night following the original Passover be a night of watching called "leyl shimmurim." [8] Passover celebrants were to watch and wait in anticipation of God's deliverance and would see how

SPIRITUAL
BATTLE · BATTLE

He watched over them. They were to remember that night and keep watching for all generations to come.

In Jesus' time, the Jews were to be alert and remember God's past faithfulness and redemption in Egypt. They were also to watch because God had not yet completed His rescue. He had promised to provide more deliverance, more protection, more of God's "watch" over Israel through His Son, the Messiah! As they vigilantly watched and waited for God's redemption that night after the Passover meal, few Jews realized their Messiah who would soon advance God's plan to restore peace or *shalom* to all things was near them, in Gethsemane.

> That night, Jesus the Messiah walked through the city of Jerusalem, crossed the Kidron Valley, and entered a garden or olive grove where there was a 'gethsemane.' He asked three of his disciples to watch and pray with him, and then stepped away by Himself, and in anticipation of the deliverance that was to come, He poured His heart out to God. Not long afterward, he was arrested, and on the very day that His people were watching and waiting for their Redeemer, he offered himself as the sacrifice for all mankind! [9]

While the three (Peter, James, and John; Matthew 26:37) should have been watching, they slept. It would have been better for Peter if he had done as Jesus asked and used this time more productively; he

SPIRITUAL
BATTLE BATTLE

might have been ready to resist Satan when challenged at Jesus' trial before he denied the Lord.

So, fellow Christian soldiers, as we wait and watch for the Lord's return, be on guard and alert to defend against Satan's attacks. Indeed, He will come after us! "But the day of the Lord will come as a thief in the night; in the which the heavens will pass away with a great noise, and the elements shall melt with fervent heat, the earth also and the works that are therein shall be burned up" (2 Peter 3:10). "And the world [i.e., satanic system] passeth away, and the lust thereof: but he that doeth the will of God abideth forever" (1 John 2:17, KJV).

Dick Savage

U.S. Army, Retired

Email: frank8050@att.net

EPILOGUE

SPIRITUALLY WOUNDED WARRIORS

Well, there you have it. Chapter after chapter breaking down the Christian warrior's spiritual battle armor or battle rattle of Ephesians chapter six, how to wear and use it. Hopefully, throughout these chapters, we introduced (or re-introduced) some valuable insights that you perhaps not thought of before and that we have challenged you to "put on the whole armor of God" After all, who would go into battle only half-dressed? Or three-fourths dressed, for that matter? What piece would be so unimportant as to leave out? Surely not the helmet or the body armor. Maybe the shoes? Ephesians 6:15 states, "having your feet shod" (KJV). Perhaps it is more than just about the shoes. So, what about socks? Who needs 'em? Ever hear of trench foot? The point is this: every part of the armor has a role to play in protecting the vital areas of your body from damage, disease, and death.

This analogy speaks plainly to our spiritual life as well. God has designed every armor piece to work in concert to provide defensive and offensive capability against our spiritual enemies. With every encounter with war comes wounds, injuries, and yes, even casualties. Are you wearing you *entire* battle rattle?

Have you ever experienced ill-fitting equipment or garments? If so, it is the last thing you reach for, or probably not at all. Because it just does not feel right, or you think it makes you look a certain way, you do not care for it. I have lots of T-shirts, jeans, etc., that fall into this category. You probably do as well.

As you have read through this book, each piece of armor was discussed in detail by ten different military veterans who have "been there, done that" while faithfully serving their God and country. What piece or pieces fit okay? These are your go-to's. For some, it might be prayer; for others, it might be Bible study, or maybe you are very secure in your faith just knowing that God is in control and it will work out in the end. What about that piece that does not fit so well? It could be the same ones mentioned above for some folks or some other element. It seems that we cannot work those armor parts into our life; we come up with lots of reasons (excuses, perhaps?), I am sure. Guess what? Those points of weakness will become the source of future wounds and injuries; if left untreated, they will be the spiritual death of you.

Chapter Three was all about knowing your enemy; about gathering "military intelligence." I am sure you know that is not just a tactic we are using. The enemy has been around for a looooong time. Don't you think he has learned a thing or two about what makes you tick? Imagine an invisible being following you around for the last year (read

Job 2:2). What would he have learned about your strengths and weaknesses? What did he see you staring at, reading, or computer surfing through? What did he see you doing when you were all alone and, in a place, where no one knew you? He would have learned a great deal about me and my struggles and have valuable information to use to his ends (John 10:10).

Those ill-fitting pieces of armor—the enemy sees that and uses it to craft his snares. We become spiritually wounded in the fight. The enemy is working to take us out, and his patience is immense. His strategy is as old as time itself—divide and conquer. It is a strategy used by both sides because it works! Deuteronomy 7:22 reads, "And the LORD your God will drive out those nations before you little by little; you will be unable to destroy them at once" (NKJV). If you read Joshua's book from a military strategist's perspective, you will see it. When the Israelites crossed the Jordan River, they took the country's central part first, dividing the enemy into north and south regions, and proceeded from there to conquer the land with God's leading. The enemy tries to do the same thing to us—isolate, cut us off, make us feel like we are the only ones dealing with stuff in our lives and that no one will understand or even be judgmental about it. Sadly, it is practical and working in the church all too well. We have walking-wounded among us.

But God has it covered! We do not need to be afraid or shamed into silence. Take heart in this verse: "Do not be afraid of those who kill the body but cannot kill the soul. Rather, be afraid of the One who can destroy both soul and body in hell" (Matthew 10:28). I know—strange verse, perhaps. God does not want to destroy us either; in fact, He has gone to great lengths not to and to make a way for me and you to escape that spiritual destruction.

Specific to the message here is this: what is the best sight in the world when you are lying wounded on the battlefield, bullets whizzing around you, shells exploding, and people yelling? Your buddy sprints towards you, pulling you to safety, and cries for the medic. You have seen it in the movies: it is a *Hooah* (Army), *Oorah* (Marines), *Hooyah* (Navy), and *Hoorah* (Air Force) moment when you know you will not be left behind.

Battle buddies. God, as always, has first dibs on this. Jesus modeled many things for us during His time walking through His creation. He picked out twelve ordinary, blue-collar guys and then got very close to three of them. He depended on them during many trying circumstances, even as He tried to teach and strengthen them for the journey ahead.

SPIRITUAL
BATTLE BATTLE

When the church came into existence, God used the same concept to help each of us. We cannot go it alone. Remember those ill-fitting pieces of armor we talked about earlier? Your battle buddy might be the one to fill in the gap, to have your back in that weak area until you have strengthened that area of your life. Look for like-minded people who are armored-up and standing firm, who know the enemy; who have a good grasp of truth; who have their feet firmly planted, ready to go; who have a powerful shield of faith; who are secure in their salvation; who knows where they are going and how to get there; who are Conan warriors in the using their swords; who are prayer-warriors, knowing the Father intimately; and who is on alert, standing watch and got your back or soul. No one person has it all down perfect, but you will have a few friends that will help cover the gaps or vulnerabilities in your armor.

Maybe you have heard of the "one another" passages. These are the ones that encourage us to buddy-up and armor-up each other. Consider these Bible passages:

"Regard one another as more important than yourselves" (Philippians 2:3).

"Confess sins to one another" (James 5:16).

"Bear one another's burdens" (Galatians 6:2).

"Speak truth to one another" (Ephesians 4:25).

"Do not lie to one another" (Colossians 3:9).

"Comfort one another" concerning the resurrection (1 Thessalonians 4:18).

"Encourage and build up one another" (1 Thessalonians 5:11).

"Stimulate one another to love and good deeds" (Hebrews 10:24).

"Pray for one another" (James 5:16).

"Be hospitable to one another" (1 Peter 4:9).

"Bear with and forgive one another" (Colossians 3:13).

Another verse that is seldom (if ever) used when we discuss the "one another" passages come from the Old Testament: "As iron sharpens iron, so one person sharpens another" (Proverbs 27:17, NIV). If we struggle with some weakness in our lives (a chink in our armor), we need our battle buddies. And the time to build those relationships is *now*—*today*. Start being intentional about it. When you are lying wounded on the battlefield, looking for that soldier-medic to come running to you, that is not the time to guess or hope for someone to come.

How does that happen? Take those eleven verses listed above and then use them to put flesh and bone on Proverbs 27:17. It is that *simple*

and yet, that *hard*. These are not pie-in-the-sky, do 'em if you feel like it, type of verses. Do you want battle buddies that will have your back in the fight of your spiritual life? Start here! Countless pages and books have been written on these on the concepts of Ephesians 6:10-18, yet they are not hard to understand. Doing it with others in a community of believers, day-in, and day-out will occupy your best time and effort. The journey will oh-so be worth it! Someone once said: "Never doubt that a small group of committed people can change the world. Indeed, it is the only thing that ever has."

Darren Crowden

U.S. Air Force, Retired / Department of Army Civilian

Email: nerrad@yahoo.com

(EDITOR'S NOTE: Darren graduated from Amridge University in Montgomery, Alabama with an MA in Mental Health Counseling with a concentration in Sexual Addictions.)

ENDNOTES – WORKS CITED

PROLOGUE

1 *Battle Rattle*. https://www.waywordradio.org/battle_rattle/
2 "Your Afghanistan Briefing," *Army Times Publishing Company*, December 14, 2009, p. 20
3 *Fight Tonight*. https://www.foxnews.com/politics/biden-defense-secretary-north-korea-warning
4 *Battle Rattle*. https://www.globalsecurity.org/military/ops/iraq-slang.htm

CHAPTER ONE, GOD'S ARMY STRONG!

1 *Dunamis*. https://biblehub.com/greek/1411.htm
2 *Explosives*. https://www.atf.gov/resource-center/fact-sheet/fact-sheet-national-center-explosives-training-and-research-ncetr
3 *Modern Military Force Structures*. https://www.cfr.org/backgrounder/modern-military-force-structures
4 *Centurion*. https://britannia.com/topic/centurion-Roman-military-officer
5 *Hood*. https://en.wikipedia.org/wiki/John_Bell_Hood

CHAPTER TWO, ARMOR-UP

1 *Stand*. https://www.lexico.com/definition/stand
2 *Hang*. https://www.ushistory.org/valleyforge/history/franklin.html
3 *Principles*. http://www.clausewitz.com/mobile/principlesofwar.htm

CHAPTER THREE, MILITARY INTELLIGENCE

1 *Duties.* http://www/military-school.org/Military_Jobs_Careers/ Intelligence/Specialists.asp

2 *Intelligence.* https://www.britannia.com/topic/intelligence-military

3 *Intelligence.* https://www.britannia.com/topic/intelligence-military

4 Mark Kelly. *How Satan Fights: A Military Intelligence Analysis of the Spiritual War.* Inspiring Voices. Bloomington, IN, 2013, pp. 80-83

5 Kelly, *How Satan Fights.*

6 *Defense Intelligence Agency.* https://www.dia/mil/About/

7 *Defense Intelligence Agency.* https://www.dia/mil/About/

8 Boole, Marla. *Spiritual Mapping.* https://www.kairostransformation.org/ Apps/articles/web/articleid/14028/columnid/2618/default.asp

9 *Struggle.* https://biblehub.com/greek

10 *Rulers.* https://biblehub.com/greek

11 *Powers.* https://biblehub.com/greek

12 *World* forces of darkness. https://biblehub.com/greek

13 *Spiritual.* https://biblehub.com/greek

14 *Wickedness.* https://biblehub.com/greek

15 *The Devil.* https://www.history.com/topics/folklore/history-of-the-devil

16 *Heavenly Places.* https://biblehub.com/greek

17 Tonilee Adamson, and Brooks, Bobbye. *Spiritual Warfare.* https://www.biblestudytools.com/bible-study/topical-studies/spiritual-warfare-lesson-2-the-strategies-of-satan-11580094.html

18 *Guerilla warfare.* https://en.m.wikipedia.org/wiki/Guerilla_warfare
19 Kozikowski, Kara E. *Guerilla Warfare.*
https://www.battlefields.org/learn/articles/guerilla-warfare
20 *Smoke Operations.* https://www.globalsecurity.org/military/library/
policy/army/fm/3-50/Ch1.htm
21 *Blind.* https://biblehub.com/thayers/5186.htm
22 Kelly, *How Satan Fights,* pp. 82-83
23 Kelly, *How Satan Fights*, pp. 82-83

CHAPTER FOUR, WEB GEAR

1 *Web Gear.* https://olive-drab.com/
od_soldiers_gear_ww2webgear.php
2 Bishop, M.C. and J.C.N. Coulston. *Roman Military Equipment from the Punic Wars to the Fall of Rome.* 2nd ed. edition. Oxford: Oxbow Books, 2006, p. 106
3 Merida, Tony, Daniel L. Akin, and David Platt. "Exalting Jesus in Ephesians." *Christ-Centered Exposition Commentary.* Holman Reference, Nashville, 2014, np
4 Neufeld, Thomas R. *Ephesians: Believers Church Bible Commentary.* Herald Press, Waterloo, Ontario, Canada. 2002, p. 300

CHAPTER FIVE, BOOTS ON THE GROUND

1 *Boots on the Ground.* https://en.mwikipedia.org/wiki/
Volney_F._Warner

2 *Territory*. https://www.goodreads.com/quotes/81703-enemy-occupied-territory---that-is-what-this-world-is-christianity-is-the

CHAPTER SIX, MISSILE DEFENSE

1 Card, Michael. *Mark the Gospel of Passion*. InterVarsity Press, Downers Grove, IL, 2012, p. 115

CHAPTER SEVEN, BONE DOME

1 *History*. http://www.historyofarmor.com/armor-history/history-of-helmet/
2 *Helmet*. https://renner.org/the-helmet-of-salvation/
3 *Helmet*. https://renner.org/the-helmet-of-salvation/
4 *Take*. https://www.merriam-webster.com/dictionary/New%20World

CHAPTER EIGHT, WEAPON TRAINING

1 Polycarp, *Martyrdom of Polycarp*. 2:4-3:1
2 Eusebius, *Church History* V.1
3 Brig. Gen. Rupertus, William H. "Marine's Rifle Creed." *Marine Corps Chevron*, March 14, 1942, https://www.usmc.edu/Research/Marincorps-History-Division/Frequently-Requested-Topics/Marines-Rifle-Creed/

CHAPTER NINE, SECURE NETWORK

1 *The Next Frontier of Military Communications.*
https://defence.nridigital.com/global_defence_technology_may19/
the_next_frontier_of_military_communications
2 *Next Frontier*: https://defence.nridigital.com/
global_defence_technology
3 *Requests.* https://biblehub.com/greek/1162.htm

CHAPTER TEN, GUARD DUTY

1 Wilson, James L. *Principles of War.* Christian Books, Annapolis, MD, 1964, p. 29
2 Mayhue, Richard. *Unmasking Satan.* Victor Books, Wheaton, IL, 1989, p. 12
3 Beam, Joe. *Seeing the Unseen.* Howard Publishing Co. West Monroe, LA, 1994, p. 15
4 Chafer, Lewis Sperry. *Satan His Motives and Methods.* Zondervan Publishing House, Grand Rapids, MI, 1919, pp. 43-50, 128
5 Chafer, *Satan His Motives and Methods*
6 Lewis, C.S. *Bad Eggs.* http://www.essentialcslewis.com
7 *Watchman.* https://biblehub.com/hebrew/6822.htm
8 *Watching.* https://biblehub.com/hebrew/8107.htm
9 Vander Laan, Ray. *The Path to the Cross Discovery Guide.* Zondervan Publishing House, Grand Rapids, MI, 2010, pp. 233-34

APPENDIX A

MILITARY JARGON/ABBREVIATIONS

APO	Army Post Office
CINC	Commander-in-Chief
CONUS	Continental United States
COP	Combat Outpost
DPO	Diplomatic Post Office
EAOS	End of Active Duty Obligated Service
ETS	Expiration Term of Service
FILBE	Family of Improved Load Bearing Equipment
FOB	Forward Operating Base
FPO	Fleet Post Office
IED	Improvised Explosive Device
MILMIN	Military Ministry
MOLLE	Modular, Lightweight, Load-carrying Equipment
M.O.R.E.	Military OutReach Encouragement
NATO	North Atlantic Treaty Organization
OCONUS	Outside Continental United States
OPS	Operations
PSYOPS	Psychological Operations
PT	(Physical Training)
ROTC	(Reserve Officer Training Corps)
SACEUR	(Supreme Allied Commander Europe)
SHAPE	(Supreme Headquarters Allied Powers Europe)

APPENDIX B
BIBLE VERSIONS/ABBREVIATIONS

ESV   English Standard Version

KJV   King James Version

MSG   The Message

NASB   New American Standard Bible

NIV   New International Version

NKJV   New King James Version

NLT   New Living Translation

PHILLIPS   J.B. Phillips New Testament

RSV   Revised Standard Version

Made in the USA
Columbia, SC
26 May 2022

60803504R00087